I'll Call You Tomorrow,

and Other Lies Between Men and Women

I'll Call You Tomorrow,

and Other Lies Between Men and Women

ERICA ABEEL

WILLIAM MORROW AND COMPANY, INC.
New York   1981

Library of Congress Cataloging in Publication Data

Abeel, Erica.
    I'll call you tomorrow, and other lies between men and women.

    1. Interpersonal communication. 2. Sex role—United States. 3. Etiquette—United States.
4. Dating (Social customs I. Title.
HM132.A22   306.7   81-9520
ISBN 0-688-00675-2   AACR2

Printed in the United States of America

First Edition

1 2 3 4 5 6 7 8 9 10

To Maud and Neilson

Acknowledgments

Grateful acknowledgments to: Nancy Newhouse, Pat Golbitz, Carol Rinzler, Jack Nessel, Jim Barden, Ilene Barth, Betsy Cenedella, Susan Edmiston and Judith Daniels.

Contents

I'll Call You Tomorrow,

and Other Lies Between Men and Women

Manspeak

My friend Xenia believes that lack of communication about "promises" to call is the largest small problem between men and women today. The most sensible woman is liable to come unhinged when a man of substance showers her with adulation—then fails to follow through. He admires her work, her beauty without glasses, her rapport with her children, her spontaneity. Things have never come together quite this fast. On a scale of one to ten this one's a fifteen. Just one hitch: There's no sequel.

Consider the experience of Dottie, bizarre in its particulars, but all too common in its denouement. Behind the gleaming samovars of the Russian Tea Room, she is renewing old ties with Alfie, a lawyer who has recently discovered that doing well is a better revenge than doing good. The moment has a certain urgency: Dottie is about to leave for the Coast on business. Alfie suggests meeting in Beverly Hills. Despite his ardor and the visions of new lingerie dancing in her head, Dottie is torn: Is she dexterous enough to combine dalliance with business? After two days of soul-searching, she decides to hold the dalliance until her return. She only dreads having to disappoint Alfie. She never has to. She never hears from him again. (Postscript: Not one to mope around, Dottie calls Alfie to find out wha' hoppen. He was felled by laryngitis, he mumbles.)

For Dottie the experience eerily calls up other voices, other tearooms: the fellow in brain research massaging her brain with "I sense I've met someone really special." The shrink murmuring, "With you I've decided it's different." Another beau conjuring spring in Rio. Another breathing, "I didn't know it could be like this. . . ." "I love strong women. . . ." "Call you in the morning. . . ." All gone, these enthusiasts, without precisely having come.

Now I know it's the moment for sexual rapprochement, and carping at men is tired stuff (besides, it produces poor results). But would someone please tell me what's going on?

Men are running scared, you say. Intimacy is so threatening, the moment he *feels,* opens up and drops his guard —he drops his woman.

But perhaps the problem is really a conflicting approach to language. Women, by and large, are literal-minded enough actually to mean what they say—if Dottie proposes to meet someone in Beverly Hills, Rio or even the corner deli, she fully intends to, bless her. But men of Alfie's stripe, particularly in coed situations, deploy language more fancifully. One could label their seductive, high-flying jargon "Manspeak."

Without being divisively judgmental, and in the spirit of disinterested research—like Margaret Mead's among the Samoans—one might well ask: Why the hell do they do it?

Hypothesis #1: It is entirely possible, I believe, that users of Manspeak don't experience themselves as duplicitous. Simply, they belong to what Jung called the "discontinuous" type, a charitable title for someone with the memory of a fruit fly. While the "continuous" type, according to Michael Malone in *Psychetypes,* "believes in verbal consistency," feeling "distress if the past is invalidated," the "discontinuous" type has "a weak sense of the past," perceiving it as "insignificant."

Thus, because of his feeble sense of the past, Alfie might forget the California plan somewhere between the Tea Room's revolving door and Fifty-seventh Street, while two days later spoilsport Dottie would feel distressed when Alfie doesn't call on account of her "verbal consistency" hang-up. Alfie wouldn't, however, consider a client's fee insignificant merely because it had been arrived at in the past—this flexibility is one of your handier aspects of discontinuity.

This "discontinuous" type, moreover, "easily gets involved in whatever is presented at the time regardless of prior involvements or long-term situations." So a prior involvement, like a wife, might become obscured by whatever is presenting at the time, like Dottie, until she, too, becomes prior. The only major drawback being that the priors are apt to conclude Alfie is an irresponsible swine when he was only being Totally Discontinuous.

Hypothesis #2: When employed to flatter and seduce, Manspeak is a vestigial form of the "line." As an appendix or tonsils once performed a useful function, so, back in the pre-*Grease* era, sweet talk greased the way. Today, though, She is likely as willing as He and requires neither unctuous praise nor false promises—so the line is superfluous, luffing unwanted in the breeze. But just as the appendix continues to hang in, so the fellow in heat continues to emit lines.

Though much less endearing, the linesman reminds me of my dog. Before bedding down, he turns several circles on the rug through some body-memory of ancestors flattening the prairie grass.

My friend Norman, however, assures me that Manspeak is still a vital ingredient of courtship. Though a fellow can reasonably expect to score, Manspeak, like the Concorde, speeds him to his destination. Anyway, says Norman, the badinage, the game, is the fun part (which may be disappointing news to those like Dottie who don't know from games, or liberationists who want to say goodbye to all that). Above all, says Norm, a man enjoys overcoming her resistance and triumphing where others have failed, locking antlers, in his imagination, with herds of prior thwarted swains. "The pleasure," asserts Norman, "is in the act of seduction, not copulation." Which strikes me as very refined, not to say Continental.

Hypothesis #3: Manspeak functions as a verbal form of masturbation, which, in the age of sexual Joy, has seen a dramatic resurgence. It's especially adaptive for the married or spoken-for man encumbered by "prior involvements": He can diddle himself with seductive language and get high as a kite on Romantic Possibility—without ever having to come through significantly. Eat his cupcake, so to speak, and not have it too. Women, of course, are far too prosaic to appreciate such uncommon delights.

But the pursuit of Romantic Possibility is actually a pragmatic approach to life: Giving a woman the illusion she will figure importantly in his life is a type of layaway plan, a down payment against bleaker times. For a fellow can cash in months later, or so he expects, when presumably she will still be on hold, ever hopeful.

Hypothesis #4: My friend Xenia advances yet another theory: With a certain rigidity, a man carries into his personal transactions the language and formulas of business.

When he tells Max in Sales, "I'll get back to you later in the week," he means, "some time in the dim future"—exactly the way Max hears him. Similarly, when he tells a woman, "Call you tonight," he could mean any time from 8:00 P.M. to never. But unlike Max, she, alas, is a literalist.

Hypothesis #5: Angeline disagrees with Xenia. Above all, she feels, men have a hard time giving women the bad news. They fear inordinately women's anger, a confrontation of any sort—and the "Gosh it was wonderful"s and "I'll call you soon"s ensure a hassle-free getaway. Seen charitably, Manspeak is a clumsy form of consideration, designed to let the woman down easy. No need, since civilized intercourse thrives on ellipses, to spell it out.

The question arises: Should women, besides resisting the impulse to buy peekaboo teddies at the first hint of ardor, attempt to crack the Manspeak code? Devise a crib for translating lines laid on them in the course of an average season (summer being the worst because it brings out lines as humidity does mushrooms).

"Let's elope to Brazil," for example, could be heard with the amendment: "If something else doesn't come up." "You're special," might mean: "Like human beings and snowflakes, none of which the Lord created identical, and until dawn." "It wouldn't be fair to get involved with you until I've resolved my feelings for my wife" might be decoded as: "If my wife takes me back it's off, and if she doesn't we can still get it on."

But the forms of Manspeak are various, and it's hard to keep a clear head in its presence. More efficacious, perhaps, might be a sound-scrambling minidevice that would convert Manspeak the moment it starts befouling the environment, into a sort of classy Muzak—Gluck one time, operatic highlights the next—so the listener wouldn't have to deal with the stuff at all. And once the ersatz ardor ran its course, a pair could resume conversation, no muss, no fuss, and pursue the ramifications of the latest rise in interest rates.

As for all the "I'll call you tomorrows's," any woman who values her sanity should discount them as so much linguistic static and consider a phone solely an instrument of business.

Randy Jane

Out of circulation since a year ago Christmas and stalked by animalish urges, Jane asked around among her friends not hoarding men if they knew any suitable ones. They answered no. Finally Xenia the worldly said she did know a man who was in town from Minneapolis, where he was a part-time surrogate for a sex clinic. Should she, Xenia asked Jane, send him round? Though in no position to be difficult, Jane unhesitatingly answered no. Maybe. Jane reflected, here at last was the bottom line difference between men and women: A needy (or greedy) man might resort to a lady of pleasure or free-lance surrogate (even enjoying it, to judge by testimonials). But a needy woman would stop just short of corresponding expediencies, which, to be sure, aren't often available, there being no call for them except among characters in *The Delta of Venus*.

Then, too, Jane just couldn't picture a surrogate in her living room. The children in their pajamas would tootle in with a trayful of assorted teas, offering the surrogate a choice of Pelican Punch or Red Zinger, straight up or with honey, then show him their *Faeries* book, and—oh dear, *no.*

Pleased to have by-stepped neurotic indecision, Jane had yet to solve, like so many women, the larger problem: how to manage a libidinous appetite over which she had as much control as Phaeton over the maddened steeds of Apollo's chariot.

Male sex drive, without an object of its affections, is a widely acknowledged fact of life, respectable even, catered to in the best neighborhoods. But female sex drive without an object is not nearly so acceptable as today's verbal egalitarianism might suggest. In fact, female sexuality is thought not to exist at all until summoned by a princely embrace. (Perhaps this misapprehension is encouraged by the fact that there's no icon of female lust equivalent to a man's.) And if it does exist? Unseemly, sordid, inadmissible. Women still do not have permission to be abstractly sexual—and women themselves often withhold the permission.

Jane's friends, for example, wonder why she can't just concentrate on career and children; they call her a man junkie. And when Jane says that Freud was mistaken, that she's unable to sublimate libido into creativity, that she's more creative when gratified, her friends say: Pshaw, it's love you want, not sex (No, protests Jane, for now it's sex); or they say, Think of all the women who went through the war.

Of course, anatomy is, if not destiny, a factor: Men, said Freud, are born with more libido than women are. In adolescence, concurs the sex therapist Helen Kaplan, the male sex drive is the more powerful. But by forty, that drive is subsiding; he is becoming, she said, "more stimulus-dependent, more easily dissuaded." While the woman's drive, at forty, is peaking. And since blessedly exempt from man's curse, the performance imperative, she may well have a greater potential for sensuous pleasure than he.

You'd think that the sensuous woman, perking with potential, could actively instigate encounters of the close kind. Doubtless, men of the age of John Travolta would welcome such overtures, and an occasional riper fellow might, too, if only because (a) it relieves him of the relentless burden of taking the initiative (although at least that consumed calories); (b) it's flattering, especially if he's no Robert Redford; and, best of all, (c) he wouldn't, for once, risk rejection.

But many more men find a sexually assertive woman pushy, or at best "amusing." For a stubbornly entrenched etiquette sentences women to passivity. Let's not be deluded by literary licentiousness. If the lusty heroines of *Blue Skies, No Candy, Scruples* or *Sweet Savage Love* stepped off the pages into the world, frankly pursuing gratification, they'd be more welcome on the Forty-second Street strip than in the L-shaped rooms of presentable men. The mating dance, in which the male still gets all the fancy steps, is not very different from the way Freud's disciple Marie Bonaparte perceived it some fifty years ago: "The role of everything female, from the ovum to the beloved, is a waiting one."

But some women lack a vocation for waiting. Like Randy Jane, whose better-adjusted friends find it worrisome that a person of such colossal naïveté is loose, so to speak, in New York. First she flung herself at a sensitive philanderer who had bedded numerous top media women. But after much verbal foreplay, he confessed he was liberating himself from the conquest mentality and didn't want sex without love. Next she came on to an overweight wizard of finance, only to learn he was attending a sex clinic due to lack of desire.

Jane envies the simple life of the lady baboon, who simply flashes a fuchsia rump to get things rolling.

Xenia has tried to explain to Jane that unalloyed female hunger acts as anti-musk, and is not only unappealing but grotesque. That the active, aggressive men she favors want to make the moves, that she shouldn't steal their thunder, that she should, instead, seduce, invite, exude receptivity.

"*That* old game? On the eve of the eighties?" Jane asks.

"Exactly," sighs Xenia, wondering if Jane has lived her life in Outer Mongolia—"*That* old game. What your mother taught you."

But Randy Jane only finds all this incomprehensible. After all, she, like many women at different stages of their development, likes lusty men. François Truffaut was not merely wishfully thinking but right on target in *The Man Who Loved Women*; a compulsive womanizer, neither handsome nor successful, is irresistible to women. On ideological grounds, of course, these fellows on screen or off are disgusting. But women's yen for the ardor, the eagerness and, above all, the *knowingness* of the libertine lies beyond, or, rather, beneath, ideology. The flesh has its reasons.

Incorrigible Jane now stagnates in a swamp of unrequited desire. Such remedies as running around the reservoir and cold showers, because so physical, only up her libido. The world exists to suggest—from the gray snowlight of Sunday morning to the smiling complicity of last night's string quartet. She'd be better off, Jane thinks, minus her midsection, from solar plexus to kneecap, as in some Magritte-style painting.

She survives celibacy by a spartan regime. Forbidden are: baths, looking at her body, nighties, lying down, walking (it engages the pelvis, so a little Geisha shuffle is preferable), nonfatal colds (they require bed rest—but the dangers of the prone position can be mitigated by wearing jeans).

Fortunately, most women are better adapted to the sexual inequity of our times. Like Xenia, they feel aroused only when there's a viable man in their lives. In fact, Xenia is so well synchronized that her libido plummets, she has noticed, when the viable man goes out of town on business. (Theoretically, his plummets, too, though this has not been verified.) Xenia jokes that she is just like the female rabbit going hippity-hop in the forest: It only ovulates in the presence of the male.

Xenia has also explained to Jane that even after they've launched the affair, men find flagrantly sexual women taxing, the office being demanding enough; that they flee the highly sexed woman by taking refuge in sports, participatory and spectator. She, Xenia, having lived and suffered, figured all this out after a lover told her, "Though I adore your appetite, it would scare most men"—and then jogged out of her life. Hippity-hop.

Hazards of the
New Intimacy

I'm worried about indiscretion. Betraying confidences, violating privacy, airing inner linings—other people's, that is. You could say I have a nerve worrying about indiscretion, since I recently wrote an indiscreet autobiography. Yet much more than it exposed my fellow travelers, it exposed me—which could be charitably construed as honesty rather than indiscretion. Though maybe not—I'm reminded of my friend Phyllis's remark that if ever she met Francine Gray's husband, she couldn't help but visualize him from rather an exotic angle. In any case, it's precisely my own uneasy relation to indiscretion that impels me to write about it.

What really set me off was this drink I had not long ago with PDQ (identity withheld for discretion's sake), an old acquaintance I hadn't seen in several years. While detailing his marital wars over a scotch at Charley O's, he casually dropped that his wife had attempted suicide.

Now, I didn't want to know that. Not because I'm

squeamish about suffering. But what right did I have to know that? His *wife*, after all. His soon to be ex-wife? No matter. Or rather, wasn't he all the more duty-bound, archaic as that sounds, to be perfectly discreet about anything concerning her?

And wasn't it also, I realized, Margaret I was grieving for, i.e., myself? What troubled me, as I glumly eyed my drink, was the thought that my privacy could be casually violated over a Dewar's in some fuzzy alcove, and I wanted for a crazy moment to place a lock on the self I'd painstakingly disclosed over several years, not very long ago.

These living secrets that flow between two people like water through a fish's gills used to be protected by marriage. The chances were good that over forty years a husband and wife, even if they lacked space and didn't get behind their potential, at least preserved each other's privacy. But today, with the prevalence of serial sexual shiftings, resulting in what Lionel Tiger calls "omnigamy," a system in which everyone ends up married to everyone else (or having "been with" everyone else), we've lost the structure that used to guarantee confidentiality. Everyone's positioned to know everything about everyone. Suddenly your most vulnerable parts are potentially in the public domain. And there's nothing sturdier to protect them than your ex's sense of personal honor.

Honor? Duty? Do they stand a chance in the age of self-scrutiny? Think of a consciousness-raising group, think of plain Group. In the name of mental health or sisterly man-hating, a mate's nasty habits and character disorders are offered up meekly for dissection. Theoretically, at least (I can't be sure; I'm too paranoid for Group and the one CR meeting I attended struck me dumb), the confidentiality is preserved, if only because everyone has the goods on everyone else.

But outside therapy, there's no built-in incentive to discretion. Take New Couple, struggling toward intimacy. In a glow of erotic complicity, they talk nonstop about themselves. In talking about themselves they dwell insightfully, particularly if analysands, on failed love of the past.

Max, he learns, was a manic-depressive who carried socks in his attaché case: Margot, she learns, could only get it on when she was stoned. Max, he learns, never did *that*. Margot, she learns, never did *that*. New Couple ends up with a mental portrait of each other's ex as detailed as a Dürer. This exercise may have upped their intimacy—but shouldn't a personal code of honor outlive old lovers—and shield them?

Then, too, social networks are fairly tightly knit. So unless Max and Margot have had the consideration to drop dead or move to Cincinnati, the chances are good New Couple will find themselves in the same room with one of them.

Augmenting New Couple's intimacy, troubled as used bathwater, is men's liberation from strong silence. Traditionally women excel at intimate talk, analyzing the dynamics of relationships past, present and hoped for. Now, men, struggling to evolve from emotional Cro-Magnons to a civilized stage, are learning to talk personal.

Theoretically, this is good. Practically, though, it's a blow against privacy. "Strong and silent" (and ultimately unknowable, even to himself) at least implied staunch honor that protected "history." A man who was "a man" would not only be incapable literally of tallying the emotional and sexual dysfunctions of a Margot—he'd sooner throw out his football letter.

It's to this imperiled male honor that "Mrs. Ralph" appeals in *The World According To Garp*, in one of the novel's most affecting moments; after a naked (both senses) evening, sarcastically she asks Garp not to reveal *everything* about her to his wife.

Stendhal's Julien Sorel needed no prompting: He responds to Mathilde's leading question about her rival with "gloomy silence," marveling that she could ask for "a betrayal of confidence unworthy of an honorable man."

Today's parvenu might be less punctilious. His end of the meaningful dialogue might include anatomical particulars, quality of coitus on a 1-to-10 scale, rounded off with innuendos about the ex's bi leanings.

Given the hazards of the new male verbal incontinence, the strong silent types of the past take on a sudden allure. Think of the movie stars of yesteryear—Gary Cooper, John Wayne, Jimmy Stewart—their tight, bloodless lips sealed on a woman's honor. Maybe they were inarticulate, inaccessible, boorish—yet their silence was more respectful of women than liberated man's eloquence.

So how, without violating "history," do you engineer intimacy? After all, to open yourself—what the French call *épanchement*—to experience yourself mirrored in the Other is almost more need than luxury.

Phyllis suggests the Middle Name rule. When a new beau proposed they tumble into bed, she protested, "But we don't know each other's middle name!" This rule could apply equally to verbal intimacy. Instead of an instant printout of your psychohistory, or "Did I tell you what Margot's Bomber pulled today?," why not the slow, roundabout route to familiarity.

First, an exchange of views on China, marital rape, or human rights versus human obligations—easy enough to manage now that women can talk about issues as well as they talk about love. Next, a feeling out for commonality. But slowly, slowly. Finally, middle name divulged and all signals clear, you're ready to be emotionally naked together—though you'd still, by tacit consent, be reticent about Margot, Max, and predecessors. And this joint reticence would inspire trust, which would in turn foster intimacy. And if the current ties unraveled, you could at least count on discretion.

Phyllis doesn't recommend, though, the extreme reticence she encountered on a weekend with Peter Jock. When she asked anything unrelated to municipal bonds pertaining to his life before the previous hour, he snapped: "You're prying."

Parental Guidance

While there's plenty of talk these days about men and women trading roles, you don't hear much about role switching in single-parent households. In ours, for example, the children seem to feel they are my parents. I don't remember precisely when they staged their coup, but the other day I heard them outside my bed/workroom door murmuring, "She's been in there for weeks; shouldn't she get out?" as if their mother were some large pale child in need of air.

The pygnies (sic, their spelling) are especially take-charge in the morning, when Mother's hypothyroid torpor spiked with the hazards of the single life lands the egg on the pilot light. Maud, cheerful but resigned: "Oh, Mommie." Neilson (solicitously): "Go back to bed, Mom. You need your rest." But at any hour of the day they'll dispense such seasoned advice as: "Don't dye your hair, it turns green." Or: "Forget him, Mama, it's over."

It's spooky, getting relegated to aging teen-ager. I've been mothered—and fathered—before, but never by my own kids. Do I simply activate mothering juices wherever I pass? At least I'm not the only truant from maturity on the block. Some of the nicest single parents I know are just bucking adolescence at forty. But unlike them, I am expected to rise to the lofty standards of Mistress Maud, arbiter of tact, doyenne of neatness and top banana.

I know: This is the wrong place for a valentine. It's just that I always knew about sons, but I never knew about daughters. I thought they'd be cutesy or steal my act. It's just that Maud has ferocious dark bangs and knows Mark Rothko's original name without being obnoxious.

Nor can she fool anyone for long with her eight-year-old facade. She dresses the sitter for fifty-knot winds and smooths her rumpled morale, scolds me for perorating in restaurants about slow service, laughs at the "dumb jokes" of imbibing grown-ups.

But when it comes to psychological savvy, she defers to the resident eleven-year-old, who has internalized, along with countless Reggie bars, the directives in *The Boys and Girls Book About Divorce*, by Richard Gardner. If forgetfully I ask Neilson to dance, gently he declines, saying, "Mothers shouldn't make sons their man."

Just when I think the pygnies have carried things too far and should be able to receive advice as well as dispense it, they regress to childhood. In fact, they manage this three times a day, during meals. One sleeting Sunday they unhinge a door, but when mother, too, becomes unhinged—presto! they scrap the kid act, and Neilson's saying, "Sit down and have some applesauce."

Their most serious attention, though, is reserved for

the marriage question. Sometimes they protest, "Why can't you just be happy with us?"

"Grown-ups also need other grown-ups," I answer.

"You know," Neilson explains, "for smooching."

"You can smooch with us," Maud says.

"Not that kind," Neilson interrupts. "Like in *Penthouse*."

But after some debate they've come out in favor of remarriage. They like the hours. I'd be home nights instead of gallivanting. In fact, their mothering behavior, explains my colleague Dr. Alan Goldstein, is partly an attempt to make Mother an acceptable package so she'll remarry—and upgrade the quality of their lives.

The trouble is they impose eccentric conditions: The prospective groom would never smoke and he would sleep out. They've also been known to push a candidate purely for his stash of Funions and Twinkies. And their marriage-broker style would make a *schatchen* look subtle. Typical is this café scene last August:

Maud (to a passing cat): "Some people want to get married in the worst way."

Neilson (to the suitor at our table): "Get the hint?"

Good grief (the preferred pygny expletive)—they're far worldlier than I was in my gossamer childhood cocoon. When the subject wasn't roses, my mother and grandmother spoke Yiddish. As my confidantes annoyingly don't speak French, the kids are sometimes privy to steamy grown-up secrets.

Of course I, too, at eight knew all about love from *Silver Screen*'s cover of Paul Henreid and what I could imagine of *Forever Amber*, playing at Flushing's tribute to El Alhambra, and censored by my parents (I think it showed smooching). Yet that was considerably more wholesome than Maud's favorite song from *A Little Night Music*:

> I'm before him on my knees and he kisses me
> He assumes I lose my reason and I do
> Love's disgusting, love's insane
> I think love's a dirty business

"Don't sing that, Maud," I say sharply.

"Why not?"

It glorifies female masochism is why, I want to say—but I ask, "Well, what does it mean to you?"

"The lady doesn't like her husband."

Right by half. As long as she doesn't know about the half that goes with it. Still, I worry: Are they miniature elders, prematurely wizened in the brain? Wee dust-bowl faces from Walker Evans, or like the gravelly-voiced urchin in *Days of Heaven*. Should I be shielding my daughter from "dirty business," at least forestalling glimpses? Yet can we, much as we'd love to, protect them very much at all?

As an aspiring parent I nonetheless try to lay down guidelines, to instill values. When Maud triumphantly reports she has unearthed a Big Mac apple pie wrapper from under brother's desk, I intone (wondering when she'll find the ones under mine), "No tattling."

Through my example I promote, when not sneaking pies or conjuring Paul Henreid, the work ethic. They should become doctors, I tell them, so they can do good and do well in one blow, but not the sort of doctor who puts you on hold so you can listen to the "Leonore Overture," so *tacky*, and they should humbly accept house calls on New Year's . . . but darn it, the pygnies aren't even listening. This week they want to be veterinarians and commune with lemurs in Nairobi. They then observe I've been in my room for days, that "poor" Mama looks pasty so maybe we should take a turn around the reservoir, with a quick stopover at Big Mac's for an MSG heartbunger, topped off with the six o'clock showing of *Summermutt*.

Instead we opt for my choice, *Saturday Night Fever*, only I'd overlooked the R rating, awarded with reason I soon see, wishing to crawl under my seat. I emerge from the Olympia shaken and in need of PG. Now I've done it. The kids would never surmount exposure to such squalor.

Cautiously I feel them for trauma: Maud predicts a possible nightmare about the Verrazano Bridge but otherwise seems her usual joyous self. Neilson liked the Bee Gees and the dancing, period. Travolta and Co. were "wasting their lives."

"And they'll expect their parents to give them money, too." Maud adds indignantly.

Neilson dismisses the back-seat bestiality as "teen-age lust," lacking "decency," and they propose a health food pizza.

I resume breathing. Productive lives. Decency. Responsibility toward aspiring parents. Such values the children have! Where from? Does it matter? We're all doing something right.

Sexual Etiquette

Whiling away the hours in the office of a Park Avenue specialist, I noted in *Vogue* that Amy Vanderbilt's bible on etiquette has been expanded and contemporized by Letitia Baldrige.

I fretted. Even socially savvy Tish probably has neglected some crucial guidelines to manners between the sexes. With splitting up now a national pastime, and the iron-maiden rules of the fifties rendered obsolete by the sexual and feminist revolutions, we've entered an anarchic new terrain, everyone feeling his or her way in the dark, so to speak. Several areas are sorely in need of a sexual etiquette.

For example, conventional wisdom of the hour holds that it's now correct for women to call men up and ask them out. Just try it, friends. Recently I invited a man I'd met at a party to join me at the ballet. Why is it that when a woman calls a man he sounds panicked, almost . . . aphasic? "But you were with Z at the party," he mumbles. "Yes, an old friend," I point out, admiring his respect for turf. "I'm just winding something down," he offers. "I'll call you."

With the casting office refrain ringing in my ears, it's on to the next. "In fact, I'm only marginally interested in dance," states gentleman Number 2, as if checking off a questionnaire.

Good Lord, if someone invited me to a basketball game, would I say, "I'm only marginally interested in the Knicks"? What's with these guys?

I've asked. "Don't be silly. I love women to call," many men say. Maybe some mean it. Still, most men prefer to initiate, thereby retaining the adult prerogative of selection and control. To most men, the woman who calls is not so much mannerly-in-the-new-mode as hard up.

So far as I'm concerned, women's lib means nothing until I'm empowered to pick up the phone, at least half of the time, and take charge of my social life. Why not an equal initiating amendment after we pass the equal rights amendment? In the interim, women not yet lost to, or saved by, workaholism might invest in an answering machine, so that a thing and not a person sits waiting for the phone to ring.

Before either sex uncradles a phone, though, there's the thorny problem of turf. Who, these days, is available? (For what is an even trickier problem.) It is often women who maraud one another's turf, because of (1) prior jungle conditioning, and (2) a certain desperation unleashed by the unfavorable male/female ratio in New York City (when the exact figure was reported recently in this paper, mean-spirited men whooped with glee). The arrival of a New Man at a party this past summer set up seismic tremors across the lawn. Never mind that he'd come with someone. Rhetorical feminists seem prepared to jettison sisterhood for a viable male.

Even a relationship in terminal decline is no green light—unattached women should stand back until the bodies are cold. High punctilio, in fact, requires them to abstain from the newly detached male for the better part of a year, thus discouraging him from jumping from one liaison to the next without a decent interval.

Except for the most benighted, men seem effortlessly to respect one another's turf. Is that yet another expression of male bonding? An index of the respect—and fear—men feel for one another? Or the certainty that if they let one go by, there's another just around the corner?

Turf clear, male out of quarantine, another point of etiquette arises. Should he pick her up at her home? After all, he need no longer light her cigarettes or walk curbside. My friend Phyllis the arbiter admits a bias on this point; since she lives practically in Westchester, round-trip taxi fares are wiping her out. Recently she rebelled—and now sits home with her macramé and her principles.

I confess a nostalgia for the princely manners of yesteryear; bearing yellow roses, my father thought nothing of the three-hour round-trip commute when he was courting my mother. In contrast, the seventies pasha seldom leaves his lair. When he has thrown his back out playing squash, women friends descend with barbecued chicken and liniment, defying blizzards, muggers and the D train. Bad back or not, a man in New York need never get out of his bathrobe.

The ultimate breach of etiquette, however, has to do with the ultimate end of the affair. Or rather the nonending. Not with a bang; not even with a whimper. What happens is this: Alice and her new beau talk, eat, jog and sleep together—when POUF! It's your magical disappearing act. Days, then weeks, of ominous silence. Under the paisley bathrobe was Houdini?

If he wants out, puzzled Alice frets, why doesn't he give

some sign? Maybe he's down with peritonitis, I suggest. Or —wince—he wants space. (My friend Genevieve, assertive to the last, once called a Houdini to discuss his modus operandi. "Like I can't take hassling," she was told.)

Alice gives it a month; a month should be enough space for anybody. Then she understands: It just sort of slipped his mind that they were an item. Or else, to him, the sexual connection has no more significance than pastrami on rye, while for Alice, poor soul, it implies a Relationship.

But even a smaller relationship, even a brief carnal caper, implies responsibilities. Like a *mensch*, he honors his responsibilities toward his tailor, his orthopedist, his children from a former marriage. A sense of responsibility toward a woman he has made love with should not incapacitate him unduly. Punctuation is obligatory.

On another occasion, we'll discuss yellow roses.

Selective Niceness

How hard it is to get a fix on certain people. I say X is a prince; others say he's a swine. Some feel Y is rude; others find her agreeable. So who is right? Sometimes, I recently decided, we're all right. What we're responding to is the phenomenon of selective niceness: Since many people dispense niceness with discrimination, our perception of them is likely to depend on whether or not we've been the recipient of it. These discriminating individuals assume they have at their disposal a limited quantity of niceness which, if not husbanded, becomes depleted, like other natural resources such as oil or gas. So they allocate it frugally—a dollop here, a smidgen there—assessing where it will get results.

Selective niceness is prevalent throughout the metropolitan area, but it's particularly rampant at a seaside spa like Dog Harbor, where New York literati retreat in the summer to amuse New York's affluent. And where nonentities like Marlys paddle along as best they can, unaware that niceness is only for the deserving.

During a break in charades at the estate of a literati collector, she drifts toward D.J. Supereditor; reluctantly he recognizes her, since she's a friend of his wife. But kind Marlys feels alarmed at D.J.'s expression: Vacant and milky, his eyes flicker at her unseeing. Is he ill? She shudders—they have an obsessive, familiar cast, those eyes. Suddenly she remembers: She last saw that expression in the eyes of the crazed albino trying to kill Goldie Hawn in *Foul Play*.

In her naïveté Marlys failed to recognize that D.J., a model of thrift, hasn't yet flipped his nice switch.

For a moment, D.J. studies her décolletage—Marlys sees a stirring, a clouding in the milky white, as at the dawn of Creation. Then he spots E. F. Wheeler: very *hot*. Miraculously, D.J. is . . . hale again, cordial, whisking off. . . .

Wandering through this vale like some latter-day Candide, Marlys has never been quick herself at adapting to changing realities. Such as her new status this season: Her astrological cookbook is nudging best sellerdom and she's now on the map.

But Marlys, who seems to thank the world for endorsing her existence, is unprepared for the deluge of fondness. At a fund-raiser for battered husbands (Dog Harbor likes to combine operating with altruism), Marlys feels wildly out of sync with the flow. In fact, she keeps crashing into people—like E. F. Wheeler—who never recognize her. She used to smile discreetly at a spot north of his ear, and glide on. But now he pirouettes toward her, Marlys performing her double-step pass, when smack!—they collide. She needs to rechoreograph her act, Marlys thinks blurrily from the moist embrace of new friends.

The worst is, from certain friends Marlys could once count on a consistent, if low-key response—like being ignored. But these days she never knows what to expect. "How many hard-cover copies have you sold?" demands Jan Superagent at a working surf-side brunch, beaming 1,000 rads of warmth.

"About thirty thousand," Marlys answers timidly.

Jan, who is about to up the strength, remains poised between 1,000 rads and 2,000. "Only thirty? With that rave in the *Sunday Review*?" she asks suspiciously, fixing Marlys with wolverine eyes; wondering if Marlys is *testing* her; Marlys uneasy, wishing she knew where she *stood* with her friends.

Though innocents like Marlys have their trials, it's rougher on the judiciously nice. So many nuances to monitor—you need a computer for updating alone. This week someone merits niceness, the next he has been kicked sideways. And who can afford to squander charm on some nouveau nonentity?

Take Dinny, a case of here-today-gone-tomorrow. Just as her old fans regroup in the distance around a hotter item—here comes Dinny, risen again, phoenixlike. On national television no less.

Sometimes with a troublemaker like Dinny (enough to overload anyone's circuits), the selectively nice just go with niceness. It's a form of insurance, or a gamble in the spirit of Pascal's wager. Cast your lot with God, Pascal advised the seventeenth-century libertines, since if He exists, you have everything to gain, and if He doesn't, what do you lose?

But the selectively nice must also contend with insolent decoding by people more socially savvy than Marlys. One day a paranoid accuses them of not loving him for himself; next, some purist impugns the quality of their affection, even accusing them of self-interest.

So, for the sake of simplicity, some of the niggardly nice hold to a formula, such as nothing too good for family, nothing too rotten for everyone else. Though the formula is restful (there are fewer variables), it makes you appear schizy, even to yourself.

Take Harry Houdini, a famous single father and house-person. Toward his daughters he's angelic, a martyr of paternity. He's the Père Goriot of East End Avenue. But with grown-up women he grows fangs; he hardly knows himself. And a subcommittee of NOW has just taken out a contract on him.

Then there's Mr. or Ms. Nice, an angel in public but an ogre in private. (And a hoary tradition—said Montaigne, "Few men are admired by their servants.") This formula is supereconomical: Niceness to colleagues is great P.R.— and undermines the credibility of the malcontent at home.

And there's also the Do-Gooder, who is kinder to lofty Abstractions than to mere people. Like the lawyer crusading for Human Rights abroad—and squashing a few expendables in the immediate vicinity.

And what about the higher-ups? How do they tolerate so much niceness? How do they keep from buckling beneath a mortal dose of caring?

In self-defense, the powerful devise various forms of toady-proofing. These range from speech deviations to more aggressive hostility. One higher-up may deter sycophants by affecting amnesia, a lurching gait or an inaudible mutter; another by smoking cheap cigars; still another by barricading himself behind bourbon.

Sprinkled among the hordes of cost-effective personalities are the promiscuously nice. Some of these oddities are so shamelessly nice they've achieved a certain notoriety, like Marlys, who was gracious even in the hospital (which could be construed as tasteless ostentation, though maybe she was gaga on Demerol). Like that man who forfeited a cab on a rainy night. Or like that fellow overheard being charming to a Triborough Bridge toll-taker.

These hard-nosed nice, however, are privately regarded by many as hopelessly spendthrift. They're considered cranks, show-offs, outside agitators; aspiring saints, for Chrissake, angling for beatification. One wouldn't want one's sister to marry a creature so sloppy, so undiscerning, so . . . indiscriminate.

But the selectively nice have a weightier albatross: friends like themselves.

Divorce Fever

"Five years ago, when our son started private school," a psychiatrist says, "there was only one divorced kid in the class. Today the application form routinely allows for separate addresses for the mother and father."

Glamour magazine interviewed Susan and Leo Braudy because they were a Model New York Couple. They were handsome, in love, and had a dual-career marriage. The following year Susan and Leo Braudy split.

"My God, not *them*," said Victor P. over his third brandy Alexander. "It's an epidemic." Since last week Victor himself has been sleeping on a couch across town.

The dearth of apartments in New York City, Pete Hamill suggested last summer, is due to the death of marriage. When a couple splits, a new apartment is needed, and another 2 rm/ct vu is snapped up.

"Sometimes when I go to Cobble Hill to pick up Amanda," says an estranged father, "I see the other fathers in the street looking shattered. Five out of seven couples on that block separated in the last six months."

There is no shortage of evidence: Divorce Fever is raging in New York City. The fever favors a particular subculture: middle- and upper-middle-class professionals, academics, business types and media people, roughly thirty-five to forty-five years old, who are overqualified, overextended, overstimulated and, now, with the support check in the mail, overdrawn.

Divorce has always been around, of course, but never so rampant. National figures show that the divorce curve soared 82 percent between 1963 and 1972. New York City has had a phenomenal upsurge of divorce just in the past couple of years. Of all civil cases instituted here in 1973, 46 percent were uncontested matrimonial matters, compared with 25 percent the year before. Of course, the spread of divorce fever in New York is even greater than statistics indicate, because statistics don't include the many couples who are split but not legally separated or divorced.

The proliferation of splitters has made them suddenly super-visible, and now they seem the norm. He used to be an anomaly, one's Divorced Friend, feeding off cans of Hormel chili and rolling stiff sock balls around some furnished room. Quickly he was resocialized, recycled and remarried to a newer model. But today almost anybody you talk to can think right off of *six* couples who have split in the last year. That means six husbands riffling through the *Voice* classified or checking in with A Man's Share, a new roommate agency catering to recently single men; and six wives with a lot of new closet space. "In Victorian times," says Abe the Shrink, "when the going got rough, people fainted. Now they get divorced."

Model Couples seem hardly less susceptible to the fever than the predictable casualties. The fighter pairs, the pots-and-pans slingers, Ms. and Mr. Macbeth, okay. But Victor and Sally, who cuddled in a single bed? Steve and Julie, who played duo piano? Peter and Sylvia, who seemed so interlocking, so *permanent*?

In the old scenario, the husband left, or slyly provoked his wife into throwing him out. And it's still mostly husbands who leave, according to Norman Sheresky, divorce lawyer and coauthor of *Uncoupling*. But there's a new scenario emerging, though it's not yet statistically verifiable: A lot more wives are leaving, too. They storm out, crawl out, or usher to the door the father of three —with the Ethical Culture tuition statement following in the mail. Women have been the marital breakup victims so long it's hard to get a fix on this new image: the shell-shocked husband. On the Upper West Side or Bleecker Street Gardens, the wives are flourishing in freshly painted apartments, and the husband/fathers on the sidewalk look—not bitter, but dumbfounded. Like they don't know what hit them.

Everyone has his reasons, said Jean Renoir. But every couple's reasons for uncoupling are leavened by the culture's values, directives and myths. Gone, for instance, is the stigma of "divorced." Divorce is now honorable, a part of the human condition—some proselytizers argue it's a condition of being human. "Sometimes outgrowing a relationship is obligatory," says Alex Comfort in *More Joy*. There is even talk of a divorce mystique. It's like getting a Ph.D., remarks a writer in the September *Atlantic*; it's an achievement in growth and self-analysis. For some, divorce represents a necessary rite of passage to Adulthood. You have suffered, you have acted, and now you stand alone, unbuttressed by a helpmate. You are free now to develop your potential, to come and go as you like, to get laid, to buy something hideous, to not cook dinner. You are free to Start Over, ideally positioned to discover the Perfect Relationship. In escaping a moribund marriage, you have eluded death—the deathliness of nonfeeling, of rote transactions. Singleman, says Joseph Epstein in *Divorced in America*, is the new American ideal. And Singlewoman is not far behind.

With the exception of Epstein's book, whose bias is on behalf of the nuclear family, the publishing theme of the year is how to reenter Singlehood with a Panglossian optimism. Consider such titles as *Creative Divorce* and *I've Had It, You've Had It.*

Doubling the lure of the free-and-single myth is the simultaneous decay of an older myth: marriage, and such ideals as family, a shared past, security, mutual dependence, and stability. Married is something for the folks out in the Heartland, where husbands are off in the shop and wives are "the girls" gossiping over a second cup of coffee. Who in our New York subculture besides Annie Roiphe waxes romantic on the subject of the nuclear family? Her views, she has correctly observed, are considered "counterrevolutionary," even by her own children. Children, you say? Today their parents worry less about how to rear them than about where to deposit them.

The words My Wife, My Husband, stick in the craw hereabouts: They have unfashionable connotations of *ownership.* A long-term marriage is suspect, disreputable. Henry and Annette are plainly *stagnating*—in a swamp of orthodontia bills, mechanical sex, symbolic quarrels staged nightly like music hall routines, all the cues, all the one-liners known—for to grow (new myth) clearly means to grow apart. Over-fifteen-year marriages seem like some fusty corner of the Smithsonian.

The tepidness of married life is epitomized in lousy sex, which is less cause than symptom of all else in the marriage that is lousy. A husband, in Erica Jong's *Fear of Flying,* is not all bad: He does pay the American Express bill so a wife can ball her way, economy class, through Europe. While a wife, in Alison Lurie's *The War Between the Tates*, lends herself, like an expensive library book that must be handled with care and returned promptly.

Ionesco came up with the most chilling image of all in his play, *Amédée, or, How to Get Rid of It*. A married couple is haunted by a Presence in the house: In the bedroom is a corpse which mushrooms out into the living room—first a foot, then the whole torso, and so on. What is this corpse filling the house and Amédée and his wife with suffocating dread? Their marriage.

Some years back Amédée and his wife might have worked the corpse into the decorating scheme, or stepped over it, pretending it wasn't there. But now they might dissect the corpse, with the help of a couple of therapists, and get the hell out.

In New York City they'd get out several beats faster than they might in Savannah, Georgia. For we are all "possibilists" now, Joseph Epstein laments. Even if our marriage was good, "nothing any longer seems quite good *enough*." And New York teases our senses and strokes our ego and fires our fantasy of "better" like no other town.

Suddenly you hear people talking this special language, peppered with obsessively recurring words: More, Space, Growth, Intimacy, Constriction, Mobility, Autonomy, Dependence, Whole, Halves. (If they've been blanding-out in California, they'll throw in Alternatives, Scripts, Self-Actualizing.) What *is* this peculiar jargon? It's the slogans of people afflicted with split fever—and clues as to why they've got the bug:

More. Since they had the Depression to deal with, our parents worried about more eating, not more intimacy. (By the look of things, we may soon circle back to worrying about more eating.) Even in the very recent past, couples had a high tolerance for discord, and accepted compromise and a low-grade discontent. But now a low-grade fever has set in and marriages are succumbing because only a perfect relationship will do. No one wants to settle or accommodate—everyone wants *more*.

The push for "more" comes largely from psychotherapy. "It tells people, You can have more, you can have better, you can have everything," says medical writer Phyllis E., herself amicably separated from her husband of six years. Unfortunately for a marriage, though, "more" often means more for *me* rather than more for *us*. And a wife may have a very different conception of "more" than her husband.

Phyllis had a "loving and liberated marriage." Her work, her women friends, her activism in the movement, rescued her from the clichés of coupleness—"Warren couldn't have dealt with a clinging person." But here she was, in her mid-thirties, and she felt she wanted more. Her idea of more happened to include marriage, unlike a consciousness-raising group sister who says, "I can't imagine anything more revolting than going hand in hand through life." But she wasn't getting it with Warren. She wanted a child; he didn't. She wanted more in the way of intimacy, but Warren, who has never been in analysis, was very closed off and uncomfortable with anything beyond low-level intimacy— "and who wants to live with a person like that?" Phyllis doesn't delude herself with fantasies of perfection. "Life is always a compromise," she says, "but I thought I could get a better compromise."

If for wives like Phyllis "more" frequently means great depth in a one-to-one relationship, for husbands it often has horizontal connotations: more sex with more women. "A whole group of my friends," says Abe the Shrink, "recently walked away from their marriages, saying, 'There's gotta be more to life than this.'" These husbands are leaving, according to Abe, not only in search of sexual stimuli but because they have a utopian view of life. "Emotionally speaking, these men are badly educated. Their tastes are superficial. They want happiness. But for them happiness means no problems. They've got the fantasy that if they Start Over there won't be any. Of course they can opt for an Uncommitted Relationship, like those launched in gay bars, and now very common among straights. Uncommitted is simpler—that's one of its attractions."

Space. In a marriage, people require psychological space —broom closets and secret inner rooms, strictly nonfunctional—long vistas, and possibilities for ruthless expansion. When they don't get the space, they start to give off those pre-separation yelps and gasps of asphyxiation: "You're constricting me, sitting on me, crowding me out, blocking my development." Like Cathy, who is shy, talented, undeveloped, and in the orbit of Michael, who is gregarious, witty, one of the most successful copywriters in town. Cathy starts to read her twelve-year marriage as, "He's been taking up my air and sunlight; I can't flourish in his shadow, he's too big, he overwhelms me."

In Cathy's thinking there is a next logical step: "I'm not going to change him, I don't *want* to change him—but if *I'm* to grow and develop I'd better relocate in a new space where I won't be choked off." On his end, Michael is thinking, "There's gotta be more to life than this," and having fantasies about this dark, sensual, joyous cookbook writer he's met who's just the opposite of his Cathy. Though they've come from such different places, the consensus is there: Let's split.

An extraordinary thing happens during their trial separation. Transplanted, Cathy flourishes in her new open space. Her energy is released; she connects with people, women particularly, who offer a fretwork of emotional support. She also gets two great job offers in one week, a book contract, self-esteem.

For Michael, though, there is suddenly far too much space around him. He manages to avoid a breakdown. Barely.

Dependency. To depend on the person you married used to be respectable. Marriage, in fact, used to *mean* dependency. A couple was a symbiotic unit, a neurotic double-compensation. Now, thanks to psychotherapy, dependency is a double felony—against yourself (you're a cripple) and against your mate (he's got you around his neck). The Sullivanians, especially, are notorious for viewing marriage as "hostile integration." Visit Sullivan County, between Seventy-seventh and Eighty-second Streets on Broadway, and watch analysands leaving their "sessions," determined to get home and proclaim their autonomy.

Mimi is an architect, talented and domineering. Sam is charming and infantile. Mimi takes care of Sam—without her he might not be able to get out their front door. Not long ago Mimi shucked Sam, to everyone's disappointment—they were a perfect dinner party duo. Mimi sees it differently: "I couldn't stand being the only grown-up in the family."

Peter is a designer, talented and domineering. Sylvia is charming and infantile. Peter and Sylvia are about to sign a separation agreement, and part of the reason for the demise of the marriage, according to Peter, is that he started to feel that he was carrying around dead weight. Why should he be responsible for someone else's life? Like Mimi, he couldn't stand being the only grown-up in the family.

Mimi and Sam and Peter and Sylvia were all in couples therapy—where the key word is autonomy and where the important thing, said the resident match-unmaker, is not to save marriages but to save *lives*. If Mimi and Peter wanted to throw the dead weight off their backs, Sam and

Sylvia were equally motivated—to throw down their crutches and walk. It all depends.

For thirty-five- to forty-five-year-olds, it's the timing that queers it. People who are forty or so are in crisis anyway: They reassess the past, find it wanting, realize they must Do It now instead of next week. For the first time, they see a classmate's picture on the obit page. But today's forty-year-olds are prime split material because, along with their other troubles, they got caught in a generational crunch. They came of age in the priggish, conformist fifties, when *McCall's* was selling Togetherness—but the rules they played by then no longer apply. Those rules have been revoked by the sexual and the feminist revolutions.

If you didn't marry, back in the fifties, you were defecting from the human race. Although some people married for love, many others pledged their lives for less promising reasons, frequently having to do with Mother. They had working against them, too, their sheer inexperience. As Peter puts it, "First marriages are like prisons. They happen before you know yourself very well, or what you wanted. There are so many things you haven't tried. If the two of you can broaden your life experience together, fine." But soon Peter was falling back on another cliché, telling his parents that he and Sylvia were separating because they were "growing in different directions."

Much of their inexperience was due to generational puritanism—for they were courting at a time when "shacking up" was only for Bohemians and other misfits. The sexual revolution in the sixties may have delivered the *coup de grace* to many already wobbly unions. For "lacking a wide experience of life" could also be translated "lacking a wide experience of sex."

"We were very virginal when we married—even the

men," says Peter, who is forty-one. "My friends and I had never sowed our wild oats." Sex with one's mate may be okay—superlative, for all one knows—but that's the trouble: It's all one knows. And suddenly, Out There, there's a lot of action. In an Amish village it wouldn't be hard to be monogamous. But in New York? There's a *pressure* here to commit adultery, writer Susan Braudy feels; it's square *not* to. She would say to a man at a party, "But I'm married," and he would say, "I don't mind."

The trouble is, the fifties philanderer can't sustain a mistress-and-wife combo. "If they *could* have affairs, they might stay married," says psychiatrist Richard Rabkin, who believes that saving lives need not rule out saving marriages. But this is what happens: The affairs turn out to be not very satisfactory, because either they are one-dimensional and offer just sex (Peter recalls that in six months he'd never seen Nell in the daylight), or else the relationship flourishes and the lovers grow greedy for more of each other's time, putting the affair on a direct collision course with the marriage.

But—most fatal to the affair solution—the fifties philanderer is a romantic idealist. He may be horny, but he's also sentimental. As Peter puts it, "I found I couldn't separate sex and emotional involvement. I'd come home at three A.M. from Nell and climb into bed with Sylvia and it was . . . well, disorienting. I can't be involved with two women at the same time. I want it all with one woman." The solution soon becomes painfully obvious: Pull up stakes and move on in search of her.

The embattled couple straddling two generations may have managed to Self-Actualize in tandem, may have ridden out the sexual revolution. But can they survive the feminist revolution? Suddenly no one wants to be the wife. Not the wife, certainly, and not the husband, and not the baby-sitter, though she is usually in there pinch-hitting, sullen and dreaming of an island with 95-degree weather where there are crazy fruits instead of crazy people. As sociologist Jessie Bernard sees it, every marriage is really two marriages—the husband's and the wife's—and the wife now thinks she got a bum deal. She communicates this opinion to her husband. And suddenly, without realizing it perhaps, they've become a high-risk couple. For in questioning and then altering the Starting Line terms of the marriage, the wife is propelling them toward the Finish Line.

She started playing at marriage by the old division-of-labor rules: Husband develops a career; wife tends home and children. The consensus between them on what each role entailed made for stability. But now, fifteen or so years later, the wife is caught short. She develops mad-housewife symptoms and admits to the title "housewife" only with irony. For she feels herself a "failure." So what if her husband is the Martin Arrowsmith of Mt. Sinai? Surrogate success won't wash anymore.

The husband, meanwhile, is perplexed about this sudden *Sturm und Drang* polluting the atmosphere of his co-op. For he has given his wife what he has never had himself: time. The freedom to do what she wants. Their dialogue, repeated from Turtle Bay to Brooklyn Heights, from Gramercy Park to Riverdale, might run:

He: What's so terrible about having bed, board, Bonwit's, the shrink, plus a free-lance photography career subsidized by me?

She: It's like getting charity.

He: Just check out the Long Island Expressway any weekday at five-thirty P.M. Who's sitting there? Husbands. And what's so terrible about charity?

She: I have no control over my own life. I feel like a house nigger.

He: Damn nice house, too . . .

Joseph Epstein and his wife had a very nice house. But the woman Joseph Epstein married was no longer nice. In fact, she was alternately morose, sniping, and bored. She was spoiling everything by making this impossible *demand* on him. She was asking him to make her *whole*. It was infuriating.

She was furious, too. He was part of the system that reduced her to this sorry state—yet he didn't acknowledge one iota of responsibility. Their marital ties snarled into a Laingian knot that goes: He's angry at her for being angry at him for tacitly contributing to her crippling. In time the knot was cut.

But if many couples are splitting because the wife feels halved, even more are splitting because the wife has grown whole. One West Side couple, formerly a model marriage, are now a model for marital debacle. Like so many couples, they had this "contract" that she was a wreck and that he, the brilliant young critic, would take care of her. Little by little, with his collaboration, the wreck was rehabilitated. But as she grew stronger, more competent, more successful in her own work, he in turn felt diminished. The balance of power shifted. Try as they might, there was no way to renegotiate back. Maybe the real trouble is that God can't be kept waiting for dinner.

Eventually a marriage collapsing from within becomes susceptible to all the separation and divorce without. Sometimes a row of connecting marriages topples, in slow or quick succession, like a row of dominoes. In one such nexus, a row of brownstones in the West Eighties, the first to fall were Alex and Diana, who opened their marriage so wide it disappeared. After them went their best friends, George and Nina, who hated each other. Brad then decided to console Nina and leave his wife, Lore, pregnant with their second child. The most recent to go are the hub couple of the group, Dan and Betsy, who were perfect.

People with lurid imaginations speak of contagion and epidemics. They cite a sudden proliferation of Sullivanian rabbit warrens in a building on Broadway and Eighty-second, where matrimonial defectors are given safe-conduct. They also cite a divorce plague that wiped out the whole E line in the Eldorado. Movement women, it is rumored, are prime carriers and can transmit divorce fever over the phone. Joan K., a forty-five-year-old psychiatrist who separated amicably from her husband, claims that her neighbors in Barnes Landing placed her in quarantine this summer to protect adjacent marriages.

Often the emulation of role models is a key factor in the domino dynamic. Mina Superstar is very much admired by Phyllis and Karen. When Mina separated from her husband, Phyllis's pulse quickened and she started a mental brief against her own marriage. But one reason she'd always hung in there was terror of living alone and the low probability, so she imagined, of ever being with a decent man again. But here's Mina, cut loose, and she seems to have lots of men. Mina is making a go of it. Why shouldn't it be the same for her, Phyllis?

Karen, married very young, feels sexually deprived and raring to range around a little, and she looks at Mina and Phyllis with their sexy new lives. Her temperature shoots up. Why shouldn't it be the same for her?

Some role models blow up larger than life, like a Nana doll, and become myths. Like Carla Z., who walked out of her marriage, taking the three kids with her. Carla left behind (1) the upper ten percentile income bracket; (2) nine rooms on West Eighty-sixth Street and the beach house in Seaview; (3) a husband who was a self-made V.P. with a company Lincoln Continental and who was such a wonderful father that his mother-in-law, permanently stricken by the desertion, is still cooking the erstwhile couple vats of fig compote and borscht. The story goes that *he* was conservative and inclined to workaholism, while *she* converted from Bendel's to the barricades. A detractor puts it, "Carla was always going with the latest revolution. First it was jail with the Berrigans and Grace Paley. Then it was feminism."

Whatever the reason for Carla's defection, she is the first domino in a seemingly endless row. Next thing you know, her best friend Sally is dumping Victor. "Carla ·showed Sally the way," Victor says. "There was Carla living out her liberation on her husband's money. She'd never been happier. She went back to college. She had a lover. And Sally got the message: Shed me, but not my money."

But Carla's message reaches far beyond the circle of her close friends. She embodies the fantasies of women all over the city who scarcely know her. To them she is Brave New Woman. To their husbands she is the evil genie of Feminism, legitimizing and cheering on the wife walkouts.

Carla is not unaware. "I seem to be the topic of much discussion," she says. "There's some kind of myth about me. A woman from my old building came up to me in the lobby and said, 'I wanna have lunch with you and pick your brain. You showed such chutzpah by walking out of this building and leaving your husband. And you looked like you had everything.'" The other day a woman she had never seen before told her, "I just left my husband, thanks to you."

This kind of talk makes Carla uncomfortable. She says the women who claim they're emulating her have never seen her crying in her bed; she says they've never seen her pain.

Will the divorce epidemic rage a while longer and then, like some biblical scourge, pass over? One reason to suspect its transitoriness is the accelerating obsolescence of all cultural artifacts. Moral styles may also flicker by at an accelerating speed, and the slogans of the subculture in '74 may seem, soon enough, so many fads. Split fever, too, is a phenomenon of people turning forty now. The next generation of forty-year-olds may well take for granted some form of long-term cohabitation, and the challenge of the future, feels psychiatrist Richard Rabkin, will be to make a dual-career ménage that includes children really workable.

Then, too, there is already a reaction setting in, a disillusionment with the life of Singleman and Singlewoman. Pain wasn't written into the Adult and Autonomous scenario. Yet here's the husband who walked out in search of More suddenly finding that *"la chair est triste,"* especially in an East Sixties studio; and here's Brave New Woman crying in her bed in the morning. Singles, male and female both, discover it's a mighty stressful life, this business of being "on" all the time. With a spouse, you could at least be a slob. And the turnover of lovers is dizzying. All you want suddenly is to turn over and go to sleep. Be forewarned: A strange nostalgia may set in. A recent casualty not yet on speaking terms with his wife dials her number in the hope she's out so he can listen to her voice on the answering machine. And the marrieds who left in the name of Autonomy find they wouldn't mind all that much if they could (1) depend on someone for maybe a week, and (2) find someone who needed *them* a little. Can it be that Single really means Time Out? And the solution is *re*marriage?

For the rest of the country the answer is yes. The Bureau of the Census reveals that three fourths of all divorced men and two thirds of all divorced women remarry. And they do it fast, on the average of five years from the date of separation. (In the man's case, speed may be of the essence: According to the National Center for Health

Statistics divorced men are four times as likely as married men to commit suicide.) Moreover, three fourths of all remarriages are lifetime propositions. Which is all very instructive with regard to the rest of America, but not to the urban subculture; *its* tone is more temporizing.

After the fever highs and the glacial lows, there is a new need for caution, slowness, tentativeness. A lot of casualties are acting as if they're just home from the Magic Mountain and need to clear their heads a bit before rejoining the living. So there's no rush—even to divorce legally. Some observers go so far as to suggest cynically that permanent unavailability has a certain utility.

But the new temporizing is above all an admission of confusion. There's no next move prescribed, because, as sex therapist Helen Kaplan puts it, we don't know the essential bonding pattern of humans as we do those of gibbons or trumpeter swans. So rather than opt, with ill-founded confidence, for black-white solutions—i.e., together versus separate—people are opting for halftones. Thus people who are married may live apart and find they like each other better; or live apart *un*married, à la Jean-Paul Sarte and Simone de Beauvoir; or, most common of all (check the names on your building's mail boxes), live together unmarried.

In *The Future of Marriage*, Jessie Bernard predicts there will be more of these nuanced relationships, with *degrees* of commitment between couples, on a one-to-ten scale. Perhaps there will even be some equivalent of frat pins and rings to indicate the degree. But Helen Kaplan's solution portends an even stranger new world. She likes being single again, she says, because she plans to remarry. Can it be that we'll wend our way back to that farthest-out design of all, the nuclear family?

The Losing Game

Everything was background music, for Delia the Midwesterner, compared with being successful in New York. The glamour of it, puzzling to her circle of native New Yorkers because they aspire to the country, where Delia sprains her ankle. At ten she was a junior feminist before the word was out, chafing to put Cleveland behind her and be "a contender." Now at forty she has done it: In this stately grown-up ritual beneath the motto In God We Trust, Delia is about to be dubbed a Criminal Court judge.

Off in a raised section to the right sits Delia's family. If her husband is envious, he's a good actor. In fact, Michael's beaming with pride. The only two in their set to persevere in Marriage I, Michael and Delia operate according to the grown-up equation, my gain equals yours. They demonstrate that marriage lives—secure, mature, *darling* Michael, it's whispered, being largely responsible.

Seated together in the crowded courtroom are Abby,

Marlys, Susan and Sam, without his wife, June. The women smiling, eyes too shiny, throat tight with gladness for Delia. Inductions beat bar mitzvahs and weddings, they're thinking. Women marrying work is the new taking of vows, they're thinking. But are they also measuring themselves, a bit sourly, against what Delia has put together? Reckoning the dues they, unlike Delia, have paid?

Abby the Editor, elegant but wan, like a convalescing child, stayed behind when her husband was promoted to Houston. She stayed behind not on feminist principle but because editing is what she is good at, and Houston is no book town. Of course Abby knows all about dual-career, long-distance marriage, the coming trend: She edited a book on it. But her own marriage, now over, seemed to require living in the same city. Though two years have slid by, she still mourns her mate—like a trumpeter swan. Unlike her colleagues, who don't lallygag around between mates. Anyway, she's fine, just fine—if missing a few parts, like a heart. Anyway, the men who are good at relationships (and whom she fancies) are unavailable because they stay in them. For a moment Abby hates Delia for never having been forced to choose.

Marlys was considered a dilettante, a Holly Golightly, until it turned out she had a negotiable talent. She also had a thriving old-style marriage. Then she hit the best-seller list with her astrological cookbook. Suddenly its the Donahue show, options, offers, she's not sure for what; schlumpy Marlys is tarting it up in *Story of O* heels and shirts unbuttoned to here. Suddenly Malcolm seems, well, superfluous. The phone ringing nonstop gets her high on autonomy, and aggravates the hell out of Malcolm.

Marlys proposes an Open Separation. In the game park for a season she gets a good whiff of reality: so *that's* what it's like? Packs of Amazons and a few furtive males darting about like an endangered species? And they all want to have "fun." Marlys has come to detest "fun." "Fun" is never having to give a damn. One gentleman bows out, then comes out. Another loves her success more than her body. Suddenly Malcolm seems less superfluous. At least he loved her body. These days they talk on the phone and occasionally date, which, Marlys suspects, works better as an alternate life style than a life.

Besides, dejected rejected Malcolm is now drowning in understanding women eager to eradicate his high-handed wife. Though tonight Marlys proposed more therapy, Malcolm for the moment prefers *More Joy.* . . .

Being her own person and a crackerjack prosecutor with the United States Attorney in line for Unit Chief, Susan can't even be sure she went wrong. Except she is forty-five years short of eighty-five, by which age, said a former mistress of Winston Churchill, one is at last beyond men. Her marriage with Harry unraveled while she was facing the other way, distracted by six months of work on a landmark case. Women are the brains behind relationships, she shouldn't have forgotten, and her brain had been otherwise engaged.

Somehow she'd trusted the two of them to coast, because Harry seemed so supportive about her career. So cute about her brief, calling it "the liberated woman's headache," even when she sneaked into the office on Thanksgiving. Susan now knows he thought her brief was a pain in the neck. He'd felt taken for granted—and taken on another Susan. Someone had tuned in to *his needs*, he said. He was tired of leading a stunted sex life, tired of catering to the Jewish princess as prosecutor . . . it was enough to make Susan crazy: Wives since Justinian have put up with driven, self-absorbed, absentee men. Yet when she was sprinting for the home stretch . . . and with her man's blessing? And hadn't Harry always *said* he disdained the house-hugging wives with rollaway hobbies?

Unless she found a prince like Delia's Michael, a woman couldn't win.

And what about Sam, the lone man in their pew; what does Sam want? A family man granitic in his loyalty, one of a vanishing breed, it's unlikely he'd translate itch into action. Conspicuously absent tonight is Sam's June. June mothers zealously, teaches eurythmy on alternate Tuesdays and recently presented Sam, more shell-shocked than joyful, with his fourth daughter. Sam can hear Susan saying to Marlys: "What a cop-out." Of course, in the Virginia suburb where they live June didn't have to justify her decision. But among this gang? She hadn't come tonight because she felt so defensive around her own cronies. And why should she, Sam wondered sadly. June was certainly entitled to choose her life—the trouble is, it's his life, too, after all. Remembering Harry as Susan's errand boy, frying his socks dry on the stove, Sam feels lucky to have a reasonable wife, but guilty—is June's stay-at-home addiction *his* fault?

Sam sneaks a sidelong glance at Susan: too twitchy even to notice his interest. Abby looks like a hired mourner, Marlys like a Silk Stocking hooker. But—is June, well, as exciting as these self-centered . . . witches?

After the wine and cheese, Sam and Susan walk out into the deserted streets of the court district. It's snowing lightly. They walk up Centre Street toward Little Italy. The snow and the tall loft windows, revealing brick walls and amber light, arouse in Susan a fierce craving to come in from the cold. No, she hasn't played it right, she reflects wearily. Who has? June maybe? Wouldn't that be the saddest joke of all? Well, the old arrangement was at least pain-proof. Unless the pain, for June, is still to come.

They turn into steep, crooked Grand Street. Sam talks philosophically, resignedly, about his cozy life. Describing it, Susan notes with sudden foreboding, like a set of felt traps.

Park Bench Mothers:
A View from the Shade

Spring. The phoenix and the jonquil. Breakthroughs, revolution, the rites of, whispered nothings, ogle-ins, Aqueduct, bikes, buds, Persephone come home. New Fiberglas curtains. Sap.

But not for the Park Bench Mother. For the likes of us spring is . . . parole! Six months of it, with luck. With spring I'm sprung from the apartment that winter's togetherness has made a cellblock. With the first letup of Riverside Park's forty-knot gales we're off, Neilson and I, to Sandbox City to join other parolees, dogs and the perennial perv (where does he go in winter?), hat on lap.

I collapse on the bench while Neilson stalks the box, new sand courtesy of Janet Duskin's construction-exec father-in-law—and 50-cent donations from each of us. It should be understood that I am not considered a peer. A strict seating etiquette governs sandbox society: The Great Ladies appropriate the benches facing the sun; we plebes get tan on the nape of the neck. My presence at the box is merely tolerated, although Neilson is as bellicose, clinging and whiny as the best. You see, besides coming to the park, I work. I have a job, a contract and a salary that, before the cab debacle, used to pay for transportation to the pediatrician. I am stigmatized as a Part-Time Mother.

A PTM's conversation is necessarily stunted and lacking in anecdotal richness and detail. I am often at a loss to contribute insights into bowel-movement consistency of the two-year-old, not to mention frequency and hue. My supply of cradle-death stories is limited to what I read in *Time* at the dentist's, and my understanding of toeing-in, head-banging and third trimester hemorrhoids is minimal.

By Riverside Park standards, I am a social catastrophe. Between frantic applications of Wash 'n Dri's and alfresco Pampering I just sit. The last time I read two consecutive sentences from Piaget, my son got run over by a three-speed racing tricycle; and once when I became reluctantly involved in a private school debate, it had to be pointed out that *my* child was doing something nasty in the box. It is definitely safer for all concerned if Mother is free to train on her progeny every ounce of vigilance left her after a week of 6:00 A.M. ministrations. The one activity that can be coordinated with this state is handwork. But I don't knit. (Neither do I sew, for fear my boy would aspirate the needle and thread.) Non-knitting mothers are acknowledged principally as the owners of strollers about which the knitters can wind yarn.

I may soon find myself sitting altogether in the shade.

Perhaps the worst drawback to being a Part-Time Mother is a failure to keep an accurate account of bench pregnancies, births and miscarriages. Judy Kropotkin is due sometime this week. Every A.M., Kropotkin Jr. in her wake, she waddles down to the sand box, noticeably bigger and lower. She profiles against the late morning sun, stretches, flexes, adjusts. Admire, admire. In Riverside Park, Big is Beautiful. Then five days go by, with Judy's place at the bench held vacant. And suddenly here's Judy again, relatively concave, behind a Rolls-Royce pram courtesy of the in-laws (she garages it for $30 a month since it won't fit into the elevator with the operator *and* Judy). Move over for her, ladies. Wee Sanford K., bonneted and still indignant over the trip through Judy's bony narrows, is left to his own devices. What counts is the Labor Story!

My problem is I get the sagas muddled. I have already committed several capital errors. It was Pam Wolf who had a low forceps, by the resident; not Judy, dummy. (And I thought it was a high forceps.) At Lenox Hill, *not* St. Luke's, Roberta (not Suzie?) had to relinquish her Lamaze lollies and talc and told the labor-room nurses a thing or two. And Billy passed out in the delivery room? No, dear (with withering scorn), it was during the color birth film in the husband course.

"Is Sheila still spotting?" Rhoda Berk calls across the sandbox at me from the sunny bench. I have not done my homework as usual and am about to be wiped out permanently. I shrug, fatalistic. The question travels the bench circuit. No, it's been decided, and everyone settles in for the afternoon looking put off. After all, obstetric mishaps are much kinkier than a deadly routine pregnancy. Out come the knitting needles, bottles, babies—lightly upchucking in the spring sun—juice-pocked teddies, *Woman's Day*s, animal crackers, Baggies of pretzels and saltines, Wipies: the accouterments of Motherhood.

The mommies, to the untutored eye, seem a homogeneous mix, but bench society sorts out into distinct caste-groups. There's Mommy and there's Mummy (though not many of *those* on our Radical Unchic Upper West Side), an occasional *Maman*, Maw, Mother and hey Maaaa, à la Stanley Kowalski.

Meet the aspiring-to-Dalton/Ethical Mom in Design Research bleached-out park *shmata*; proctologist's wife; pronounced biceps from rope-climbing at Kounovsky's, doing time in the West Side barrio and soon departing for points east where the natives speak English.

And her bench sisters:

The Montessori mothers who Hail Maria as they debate the merits of West Side Montessori vs. Riverside Montessori vs. Morningside Montessori vs. Bed-Stuy Mont vs. Down East Montessori vs. Little Flower Montessori vs. . . .

The kinky mother: maroon waffled hair with barrettes, Elvira Madigan dreamy in billowing white eyelet, clonker shoes, grimy heels. From some thousand-light-years-away high she breathes endearments at two nose-pickers in Tepee Town's finest and retires to the grass to practice Yoga.

The Women's Strikers: Music and Art, peace-march and grape-strike alumni; eternally collecting signatures: this week for a day-care center for Puerto Ricans. Their kids are in Manhattan Country, majoring in honky's burden, with classmates including Certified Minorities bused down from 125th Street. (Yesterday the Strikers agreed that Anne went *too* far when she adopted that black child. After all, was it fair to her own daughter?)

The socially conscious Wasp mother; Lindsay campaigner extraordinaire; husband taken for Big John at Martin Luther King's funeral, for which they jetted down. Mummy is visible only until Memorial Day, when she slips off to the Vineyard. Unlike the hairy antiwar brigade slugging it out on the steps of the Pentagon, she goes in for more genteel projects: playgrounds designed by Noguchi, balls for the Bella Vista Home for addicts, birth control centers for our Catholic minorities. (*She* has four boys and three girls. Her logic? Only people with room ought to reproduce. It's not a question of *money*, mind you, but blahblah.) With her sons at Collegiate, St. Bernard's and Buckley, her daughters at Birch Wathen and Brearley, she's all for more local control of the schools. She can be sighted dashing by the box with one of the golden retrievers, girlish and virginal in Abercrombie overalls, before whipping off for tennis at the River Club.

The whole-hog mother: no discernible aspiration, social or socially conscious, beyond being Mother. Her expression alternates between blank and beatific. She repeats compound sentences three times, softly but firmly. Wall-eyed from watching the twins sprint off simultaneously in opposite directions, permanently slung forward from reasoning mightily with Franklin in fire helmet (hard hat before Agnew), she is besieged by flailing little grimy paws and has a Thermos for every crisis. Between her knees, temporary reprieve, the family mutt. Low man on the totem pole; eyes of the Eternal Victim; thinning fur.

Finally, the reluctant mothers—*my* crowd. Part-timers, dilettantes. Subverters of sandbox morality. Self-deprecators ("For this I got my M.A. in Russian history?"). Unnatural Gonerils. Women's lib vipers badmouthing Dad. Pseudointellectuals because we tote around *The Female Eunuch* instead of yarn, have jobs, go for degrees, complain, hire nurses.

Above all, and especially above us, there is Maxine G. In every sandbox there is one ode to motherhood personified who tyrannizes her fellows by divine right, 100-proof gall and an adenoidal basso audible over a construction site. Our autocrat is Maxine, mother of Justin. She comes equipped with pronunciamentos on any subject: Welfare mothers ought to get cracking and learn a useful trade, like cosmetology; your son doesn't eat? quit your job; discipline problems? but you're bigger than he is. And on and on. Maxine never misses a day, foul weather or not, at the sandbox. There is only one circumstance that might inhibit her from making her appointed rounds: summer vacation. Reluctantly she abandons her preserve, come mid-August, to the "undesirable elements" ("not that I have anything against them"), the great teeming unwashed, descending from the high-rises of Columbus Avenue to perform undesirable acts in Mr. Duskin's sand.

Before I am lynched by Maxine and her Momfiosi, let me tell you about the children. They are, above all, *there*, having what phenomenologists call *être-là*, a presence that outshines or outshouts all in creation. They're there when you want them to be and also when you don't. In the house they object to most of your activities, like taking a shower, satisfying your most elementary needs, writing a letter, making a phone call—but are gratified and happy if you will consent to pace, just pace, with them back and forth from one end of the apartment to the other. Then they've got you where they want you and *tout est pour le mieux*, to quote some pseudointellectual. Out of the house, they lend credence to Ardrey's Territorial Imperative and dicker over Possessions: a moldy egg-carton, a half-gnawed pretzel. But they're on their own!—for a couple of precious hours—and need only to be positioned for urinating behind a tree (or on a railing, depending), a Good Humor ice-stick and a referee. After five, the situation deteriorates rapidly and all the little voices sobbing "it's mine" blend into a single whine rising from the vicinity of the sandbox. The mommies detach their sticky haunches from the benches running with raspberry ice and, reclaiming Tonka trailers and Playskool go-carts, drag children, dog, etc., upstairs for the bath.

I've left my friend Nancy for last. Nancy the park pariah. She has only one child and isn't planning another, which is unnatural, antisocial, not to say pathological. Nancy's daughter, says Maxine, is underdeveloped, like

Latin America, and must have a thyroid problem, for which Maxine prescribes Blimpie Heroes. But even worse, Nancy has been heard to say, it slipped out one day, that she . . . likes to get away occasionally from The Children! On the subject of The Mothers she is even more loathsome. "Their lives," said Nan the other day, indicating Maxine & Co., "center around their vaginas: what goes in and what comes out."

Nancy is not loved on West 104th Street and neither will I be if I continue to share the shady bench with her. But she'll make it out alive, all right; she's moving to New Milford. Not me; I'm holding my ground—although I *have* just changed my thesis topic to "Rimbaud and Nineteenth Century Infantile Politics." And yesterday I bought some needles and yarn for a nose-cosy so my son can play in the box all winter. *He* eats only the finest Blimpie Burgers. And let me tell you about Bev Hammond's labor.

A Summer with
Claire's Knee

Chances are her name is Franny, Missy, Lili, Suzi, Ali, Lizzie, Bini, Pattie, Debbie, Sharie, Sherry, Bambi or Lolly. Since the interview in March she has completed her orthodontia, dropped twenty pounds, had her acne pits peeled. It is 11:30 A.M., but she is ready now, the polish is dry, for the processional down to the beach. Dig it: Iowa-corn hang-straight hair nudging a comelier rump than ever Alex Portnoy dreamed upon, a polka-dot diaper, ten vamp violet toes. Your Mother's Helper.

Every July across the Eastern Seaboard, a quaint ritual is enacted: teen-aged girls from New Jersey and Long Island desert their families to come live with someone *else's* family, having agreed, for $35 or so a week, to help another mother sweep the ants out of the beach house and the children out of the undertow. The arrangement probably originated when someone first discovered that mothers as well as children deserve a vacation; and that budding maidens could do with a little pruning back, ideally within a summertime surrogate family. The institution often founders, however, when it is *then* discovered that the expectations of the two parties—Mother and Helper—don't quite mesh: i.e., Mother may think *she* is entitled to a vacation, but so does the Helper. Mother's Helper, it turns out, just doesn't help Mother a hell of a lot. In fact, as the summer progresses, it usually develops that Mother needs Help surviving the strains of having a Bini, Bambi or Pattie in the house.

The young ladies are usually garnered from a fat file at the high-toned Anne Andrews Agency on Madison Avenue, in which they state what they are able to do (swim); willing to do (read bedtime stories to the children); *un*able to do (housework); *un*willing to do (housework). They often state a preference for Fire Island because of its desirable working conditions: low ground cover that won't block the sun; a ready supply of bipeds in polka-dot diapers or jams; ice-cream cones with sprinkles; and the Great South Bay between them and their parents. Early in March a deal is consummated. About mid-July Mother is doing a rethink: (1) Why has she taken on the aggravations of having an adolescent daughter in the house when it's not even her daughter? (2) Since Mother, too, would rather just lie on the beach all afternoon, how can she expect Lolly to wipe Jeremy's behind, tamp Stevie's drool, hunt fiddler crabs with Cara and mop the bathroom floor, humming cheerfully? How indeed? Well, she can fault the logic of the situation all she likes, but the other options are . . . zero. So until the summer playgrounds of the Eastern Seaboard either erode totally into the Atlantic or submerge under the weight of the population, or until Rockefeller inaugurates his summer day-care program for the almost-upper-middle class, mothers will continue to hire helpers and get no satisfaction.

When there are no other options, people have a way of making do.

Fair Harbor, Fire Island. July 8. A mother-biologist-writer is making do:

. . . and if she'll only vacate the shower somewhere between 6:00 and 8:00 P.M., *free up the phone at Daddy-boat hour on Friday and keep her cronies and the . . . Grand Funk, I believe it's called . . . out of the yard when the kids are napping, I will waive the other items in our arrangement. Think Positive. It will cloud over on Sunday night instead of Friday night; the impetigo epidemic will bypass Fair Harbor this year; and tomorrow, maybe, my Mother's Helper will get up before noon.*

July 9. Noon. Debbie got in late, late, late. Woke everyone tripping over the geraniums on the porch. We are tippy-toeing about. Adam and Joely think it's a game. I am trying to Think P-P-P-Positive.

But I worry so about Debbie. All she eats, or drinks, rather, are those Diet-Rite malteds—a saving—but will she survive the summer? How is it possible to go into convulsions and be laid up for three days after eating one raw clam? Jack shouldn't have insisted . . . he was just trying to make her feel "part of the family." What will her mother say? What does she say in all those letters she posts? With two shampoos a day, she hardly gets to the beach. . . .

And the dope. "Carlie's family offers her some after dinner," Debbie says. But our is strictly grade B stuff anyway. Possibly B plus. She ate some for breakfast the other day. Ate some? What's a nice sixteen-year-old girl from Englewood Cliffs and the Dwight School doing eating dope anyway?

"She's very mature for her age, very responsible, and she's devoted to children," her mother told me at the in-

terview in March. Debbie didn't say much. I figured the scrap iron in her mouth made it hard to talk. "I'm so pleased she'll be spending the summer with nice professional people," Debbie's mother said to us. . . .

July 15. Noon. I've done Debbie an injustice. As her mother promised, she is very devoted—not to children, though, to grooming.

Start at the bottom. Toes: Paint them vermilion. Legs: Depilate, apply QT for instant tanning, with or without sun. Teeth: Apply Smile Power. Spray mouth, etc. Face: Perma-tweeze, moisturize, freshen. Apply coconut masque, sebaceous gland inhibitor, creme blusher, bronze-on acne-off. For the eyes, Wash 'n Wear Swansweep Lashes, and today, the iris contacts. Hair: Wash, sun dry, apply Love, Wella Care, Swinging Body Protein Texturizer, Bio-Kur Root Repair. Brush forward, brush backward, fondle. Hang it modestly over the bosom, doughtily down the back, jauntily all to one side. Attach Monsanto Modacrylic Wiglet.

A final all-over body cream, a whisper of Eau de Esoterica at the pulse-points, and she's ready, Debbie is, to meet her public: Adam, Joely and me. Only it's 4:00 P.M. and she looks exhausted. What will her mother think? I'd better give her the rest of the day off.

"Those teenies, those bikinis, those no-bras, those bods, and within grabbing distance twenty-four hours a day," rhapsodizes a divorced daddy grouping it at Fair Harbor with other Parents Without Partners and assorted offspring. "Wow. They're dynamite. What do you expect? It's a universal male fantasy, having a little concubine around. Of course nothing actually *happens,* at least in Fair Harbor. I once heard about some fifty-year-old guy in the Hamptons who took to the dunes with the Mother's Helper. Dynamite. What do you expect? They're fifteen years younger than your wife, your girl friend, than any-one. The youth craze, yeah that's it, the youth."

July 18. Back in the days when I was just a grown-up I used to like rainy days. They were readings days. One hardly got out of bed. It was so restoring. A mother now, I get out of bed. The kids are in the kitchen boning a horseshoe crab, Debbie has set up her escritoire on the couch and Jack is reading Lolita. *Last week he ripped through* Ada. *He's going backwards. We have a literary discussion. I say Nabokov is a dirty old man with a lot of phony erudition, and why not read your porno straight. He says Nabokov is a dirty old man with a lot of authentic erudition, and besides straight porno is boring. I say Debbie reminds me in certain particulars of* Lolita. *He says no, Ali MacGraw at fifteen. But she's blond, I say.*

"It's the Lolita syndrome," says a Robbins Rest dad and summer dropout. "Why do you think Nabokov picked an *eleven*-year-old as a sex object? Because it's about all that's left that's still verboten. With the house Lollies around here, it's strictly no touchee. That's enticing."

July 25. "The guys" are checking in. Debbie's word for her girl friends. I go into her room to see if I can persuade Adam—he's always hanging about Debbie—to forsake the bubblegum machines at the dock for the beach this after-noon. I take in the scene: an Ingres-style odalisque with granny glasses; a sea of brown pubescent skin broken by swatches of wheat-colored hair. And Adam. He looks reverential. "Oh, hi, Mrs. J." Giggle giggle. I see myself through their granny glasses: despite yoga and yogurt, size 8 and Rudi Gernreich at his minimalest, I am Esther Williams in a Lastex bathing rig drawn by George Price. "We think," giggle giggle, "Mr. J. is terrific."

July 26. Adam thinks Debbie is terrific. At three he

reaches precisely to her crotch, and since he's always hugging her, it's hard for her to get around. But Debbie's usually a good sport about it. Today they had a falling-out. He bit her on the behind while she was deep-conditioning her hair. She bit him right back—"to teach him a lesson." A cheek for a cheek, explains D., is better than one hour's worth of reason. You better believe it.

July 30. The beach is without a doubt an unsafe place for children of any age—when minded by a Mother's Helper.

Left the kids with Debbie this afternoon, so I could hike to the Sunken Forest to look at some specimens of Sassafras officinale. I never found the Sassafras but back at the Dunewood bay beach, sunstruck and guilty, I find Adam and friends clinging to a buoy beyond the deep-water markers, and Joely, sans bathing suit, munching an orange peel brought in on the tide. An otherwise enchanting scene: the girls are gamboling with the Peebles Grocery youngbloods, combing the snarls out of their siren locks, winging Frisbees, and tanning their strap marks. "Where's Debbie?" (my refrain), I ask Missy. "Oh, hi, Mrs. J. I think she's gone to look for her contact lens. She lost it in the sand." Missy's youngest charge starts fussing in its portacradle. She shifts it around, some rubberoid dolly floated in by the tide along with the orange peels and skate egg-pods, pops it a pacifier, smiles brightly at me and shrugs: babies. Debbie, it turns out, is playing cards with Dustin Hoffman moonlighting as a lifeguard, under the lifeguard stand.

"It's not that Nini is a bad kid, really," says a Saltaire mutual fund director. "And she's extremely decorative. But when it comes to getting things done, a kind of vagueness sets in. We find it's just easier in the end to do what needs doing ourselves; it takes so much more time and trouble to explain everything."

"Hire a high-school girl from Bay Shore—or any baton-twirler from the mainland—and you'll have a vacation," says a Pines CPA. "Hire a princess and you'll wait on *her* for two months. One thing holds for all of 'em: Don't pay till the end of the summer."

August 1. No crises today. I am about to pour a cassis and white wine. A shriek, suddenly, the maiden being ravished by King Kong. "It's too much," Debbie screams at me, runs into her room and slams the door. It is too much, I discover seconds later. Long fascinated by the commanding array of grooming equipment lined up on Debbie's dresser, and inspired by Fair Harbor's Poison Ivy Control, Adam is spraying hell out of the principal topsoil retainer of the island with Debbie's Feminique.

August 2. Jack seemed slightly relieved to go back to the city this evening. Is it possible? Unsatisfactory air level, Sunday traffic, and all?

Well we know what *he* does in the city when wifey and the kids are at the beach, winks *Cosmopolitan* in its July photo-essay designed to bring cheer and comfort to Single Career Ladies. The question is, what does wifey do while the m. chauvinist is at the Hippopotamus doing the funky chicken with Miss Wonderful?

When not bitching about the Mother's Helper, she is mulling over such high-level problems as how to cope with the arrival of the Mother's Helper's boyfriend:

August 11. Chuck arrived last night. Not that I mind. After all, Debbie has to have some fun too. True, we had to say no to the Davises for the second time. . . . Does he have to park his sleeping bag, surfboard, pitons, chess

*set and Navy surplus rubber raft in the living room? I
don't even like to think of it, but where did Debbie sleep
last night? Jack muttered something about tripping over
them on his way to the bathroom. What will her mother
think?*

*Chuck and Jack are talking Outward Bound summers.
Chuck admits he cheated a little on the three-day isolation
survival period and waded over to a nearby island to talk
to a friend. Jack says not only did he positively thrive on
a diet of kelp cutlets and* Siddhartha, *and soloed for four
days—he even concocted a mélange of kelp and hash to
float away the evening hours. Debbie seems suitably
impressed.*

*Dammit: Not only is my husband competing with a six-
teen-year-old jock to capture the admiration of some aging
Lolita: I am cast in the role of the Norman Rockwell
housewife complete with Swansdown pie crust, pink
curlers and canister vacuums. Never mind that I liked
Goodell but voted for Ottinger in the interests of Real-
politik, co-sponsored a Viet War Veterans' Benefit at Ocean
Beach last week, belong to NOW and wear size 8. Never
mind all that. Here I am just the same with my pink
curlers, rhubarb recipes and rolling pin.*

"It's an ersatz Oedipal situation," says a Seaview psychiatrist. "Surrogate father and daughter-helper are actually working out the perfectly normal sexual feelings which
exist in the real father-daughter relationship, but are
usually repressed because of incest fears. If a man's daughter were to prance around him in a bikini, he would probably leave the premises, grumbling about his arthritis,
when he's really worried about his erection. In the surrogate family, play father and play daughter can flirt with
the father-daughter attraction, because it's free of incest.
An adolescent girl needs validation of herself sexually.

What more natural person could she seek it from than her 'father.' If the surrogate mother understood this dynamic, there would be less friction; she would not regard the girl as a tease."

"The men fantasize about the Mother's Helper," says a Dunewood dude, "because the over-thirties don't exactly swing around here. For all the talk about sex, mate-swapping and all the rest, there's very little of that kind of action. Just a nudge or two passing on the boardwalk at night, because there's so much poison ivy on either side."

"The Mother's Helpers are so generally disruptive," says a Lonelyville professional student of the passing parade, "not simply because they're lazy. After all, no one takes that part of the deal very seriously. It's really the whole adolescent world that works on the over-thirties. The kids are so self-sufficient. They don't need anyone but each other and won't tolerate our interest in them. And that's maddening. Take *Claire's Knee:* Claire is peripherally aware of Jerome's lust, but if he were swallowed up in the lake one morning, his disappearance would not cause so much as a ripple in her universe. It's the self-absorption and exclusiveness of Claire that tantalizes Jerome. He touches her knee, he says, to exorcise his desire, but really he wants just to register his existence in her universe."

September 3. Well, we made it. No muss, no fuss, no ugly confrontations. Just poisonous smiles. Or bad vibes, as D. would say. During the last two weeks, come to think of it, I don't remember seeing her face. Just the back of her hair, squeaky clean and swinging all of a piece.

The children are napping, Jack is reading The Story of O *and I am reveling in the privacy. Next week it's F. City again. A consoling thought, though: In ten years or so, my daughter can be a Mother's Helper. And I've finally stopped having that nightmare: Debbie's mother, come all the way from Englewood Cliffs, huge, wading across the Great South Bay, shaking her fists, muttering.* . . .

The house Lollies may be more current with the latest peregrinations of John and Yoko than with the latest re-incarnation of Humbert Humbert, but snagged en route to the mainland and Englewood Cliffs, Debbie has this to say about her Fair Harbor summer:

"I think the mothers had too much trust. Wow, you should've seen the way the guys roughed up the kids when the parents went to the city. Also, well on the beach . . . well *I* wouldn't trust *my* kid with me!

"What I dug most was the time off. Some of the guys didn't get very much time off. That was really terrible. I think they were exploited. Mrs. J., though, was okay, even if she spoiled those kids a lot.

"*Mr.* J., though. He was something else again. Very together. All the guys thought he was terrific. I guess I lucked out. Missy's boss—he was always trying to lay an ego trip on her. He was nowhere. And fat, too. He thought he was really cool or something, smoking grass.

"The parents always got spaced about us guys—for one thing or another. Like where did we *go* at night, and what did we *do*. . . . Well, freaky things, nothing, like hanging around the docks. The boys used to ride their bikes off the dock into the water. Far out. But that's about it. We weren't into sex much or anything. There weren't very many personal-type relationships in the group. It was mostly just the guys all doing things together. Or rapping . . . how you can't make it with your parents. They always go and lay some number on you. . . . They *try*, but it just doesn't go down with them and us. No way.

"I guess dope was the big thing. You know, for status, like how many bad trips you'd had . . . There was a *lot* of dope around—grass, hash, poppers, coke, downs, speed, sunshine. Even Darvon. A Darvon high is something else. Some of the kids were into mesc. And skag. I've never tripped on acid. I think you have to set limits.

"But I really had a terrific summer! I'd work here again. And you know, I like little kids, I really do."

The Vintage Years

I am northbound on the Madison Avenue bus en route to Griselda the Great, underground GYN celebrity and culture maven, noted for her brilliant diagnoses in unintelligible Tcherman/American and the Japanese protocol of her office (leave your shoes in the foyer, dahlink). So I don't mind that the bus is caught in an eddy of traffic right in front of Ann Taylor's. The moment to indulge my magazine habit.

The New Intimacy, I read, is flourishing between an actress who's into Ambition and a potter who's into Nurturing.

The man next to me, I notice, is into over-the-shoulder reading.

"Whaddya know!" he exclaims. "I had an affair with that actress."

I focus my eyes straight ahead on the silver lamé leg warmers in Ann Taylor's, wondering why some people attract unsolicited confidences.

"Yep," he goes on, "she still looks pretty good."

Since he hasn't opened his *Forum,* and he's half in my lap, I murmur, "Doesn't it make you feel odd to see an article about her?" Sneaking a look: Man-Tanned and Dewar's-ad dapper.

"Nah, it doesn't make me feel odd." Then, reflectively: "After all, I had her best years."

Did he actually say that? I wonder idiotically, as the man gets up and walks off the bus.

Where I come from, men don't talk like that. They empathize, feel vulnerable, keep in touch with their feelings. They support the E.R.A. and cry. A woman is desirable, they would say, at every age. A woman's best years, they would say, are the same as a man's (especially if she's Merle Oberon, Dolores del Rio or Jackie). Well, yes. Except these very men, when you haven't seen them for a season or so, show up at a party with someone you think is their daughter.

And don't many women conspire in the same view, equating their own desirability with youth? Listen to Phyllis (forty-four) and Tom (forty-eight), laying to rest by mutual agreement a liaison of eight years.

She: I spent my best years with you.

He: God, how can you be so vulgar?

She: Dammit, I'm not vulgar—the world is.

The sequel to this dialogue is, if not vulgar, banal: Tom took up with a twenty-nine-year-old anthropologist, while Phyllis joined the legions of New York's unattached women.

Though like Tom, I, too, deplore vulgarity, I occasionally succumb to it. On birthdays and national holidays, I sense time's winged chariot. But I'm not at all sure which the best years are. I used to set them at twenty-three to twenty-nine, then at thirty to thirty-eight, then at forty to forty-and-a-half. Recently I set them back at twenty-one, because the weather turned warm and I heard a pigeon, which reminded me of Paris, where I was twenty-one with a vengeance, dragged by nothing weightier than a torn organdy dress; and because, after forty-and-a-half, I suffer a failure of imagination.

Men don't have to prime their imagination to picture life over forty—or fifty, or sixty, for that matter. True, they're devastated by intimations of mortality, and they endure the ingenious cruelties of waning virility. But unlike women, their "best years" are open-ended, and they're sexually plausible at practically any age. Think of Picasso, of Casals, of Justice Douglas. Closer to home, there is Jake; pushing sixty, he is white-fleeced, wide in the belt, wobbly in the knees and, I think, adorable. But when I'm silver, wide and wobbly will Jake think I'm adorable?

In fact, mature, a man is *more* desirable because more seasoned, established and "comfortable." Even a fiftyish fellow who merely holds a job, muddles through in the sack, and exhibits your basic human qualities will receive inordinate appreciation.

While women must log long hours at hairdressers, even going under the knife in the effort to remain improbably dewy, men don't have to look handsome—just clean. (Although a certain SoHo funk has its takers.) In fact, several women I know consider male beauty not only suspect, but a blemish. And no one envies Phyllis her new companion, who has too much self-curling hair falling into his green eyes, looks more like a porn star than a lawyer, the whole package spelling philanderer. Even moderately handsome is synonymous with intolerably narcissistic.

What's a girl to do? For inspiration, I observe a few intrepid friends. What they're doing is they're playing it like men. Workaholic and successful, they exude self-confidence and strength. Like men, their aura comes less from their appearance than from their accomplishments.

True, there are drawbacks. A powerful woman is liable to become (like a powerful man) a success-object, which is not exactly heartwarming, since we do prefer to be loved for ourselves. And the authority, drivenness and, yes, egomania of achieving women is frequently off-putting to men who want an exclusive on egomania, a satellite rather than a co-star. But often such women earn a dividend—better men.

The Intrepids are also damned attractive—and I don't mean a euphemism for spunky-but-washed-out, or some legerdemain of "style" that a Colette courtesan would substitute for firm flesh—I mean they're great-looking.

They certainly don't owe their beauty to the rituals of "feminine upkeep" (though wrinkle-resistant skin doesn't hurt), like the Page Six ladies who've contrived an ageless, anorexic androgyny thanks to Swiss face work, Tibetan yogurt and whatever it is that lies behind the Golden Door.

Nor do they conform to the feminine ideal of past generations. They've none of the languid, soft, bruise-prone vulnerability of the romantic heroine, but rather a hard-edge weatherability, a live-in face, as if in the current gender blurring they have indeed assimilated at least some of the masculine.

Whatever their chronological years, there's no doubt they're somewhere in their best ones. In fact, I'm rarely aware of their age, though occasionally I might marvel that Terry, at thirty-three, is so wise; or startle when I learn that Gina is now fifty-two. I would guess these women's allure derives from their self-image. Through their passion for work, their adventuresomeness, they've tapped not some elixir of youth but some secret of suspended ripeness. Through sheer nerve they've traveled light years from the troglodyte on the bus. We should all have such nerve.

Slouching Toward Utopia

When John Lindsay's administration created Open Admissions in 1970 and higher education went democratic, a lot of people started to grumble.

Conservatives grumbled: *Their* tax dollar was sending a lot of goof-offs to college.

Radicals grumbled: Open Admissions was really a scheme to supply industry with a college-educated low-level work force.

Professors in City University grumbled: The Visigoths were storming the academy and Taki awards would replace B.A.'s.

Medical school deans prepared to grumble: Soon they would be readmitting students through Pathology 511.

The Open Admissions students grumbled: Here they'd been invited to the party, yet no one seemed happy to see them.

When I came to John Jay College I didn't grumble

about Open Admissions. I had other problems. I had the guns to worry about.

I'd be lecturing on Flannery O'Connor's incurable diseases and the myth of Sisyphus and this glint would catch my eye: guns, clubs, handcuffs hanging off someone's belt. What if something in that walking arsenal clicked over and went bananas? There were also, I knew, *hidden* guns: around the ankle, behind the knee, and tucked snuggly into the other erogenous zones. But there was nothing for it—40 percent of my students were law enforcement officials and required by the department to be armed at all times.

Where I went to college the students didn't wear guns; they wore cashmere sweaters. We didn't analyze fingerprints; we probed our psyches. The nouveau riche daughters of Sarah Lawrence kept *their* cashmeres balled up in funky wads at the back of the drawer, and one nouveau daughter once *lost* one of the family's fleet of Fleetwoods, and in the spring we sat cross-legged in leotards under the apple blossoms reading Gerard Manley Hopkins out loud. For the spring Alumni Magazine I was photographed doing a *tour jeté* off a stone wall with a daffodil in my teeth. When I graduated class of '58, I sailed to Paris, came back fluent in *argot* and with my copy, too late to smuggle in, of Olympia Press's *Lolita* and fleas from Rue Monsieur le Prince where Richard Wright lived. I went the publishing route, got laid off when Grove Press opted for planned bankruptcy, got graduate degrees in Comparative Literature and taught some ten years at Barnard and Columbia. So John Jay was a jolt nothing short of apocalyptic.

Eventually I got used to the guns, which freed me to worry, like everyone else, about Open Admissions. But I soon picked up some exciting vibrations. A couple of professors were putting together an innovative mini-college within John Jay that would serve as a pilot for City U. and seriously test the Open Admissions proposition. *Could it really work?* The answer would determine not only the future of higher education but the fate of a very large number of the city's disadvantaged, and consequently the fate of every New Yorker.

A new educational game plan was needed for students who lacked not only reading and writing skills but the middle-class indoctrination in the liberal arts: The Leonardo in their world might well be a graffiti artist working the IRT express line and the Lévi-Strauss a slumlord in Ocean Hill-Brownsville. Why not plug them into a theme that would fuse *their* life experience with a year's worth of interconnecting seminars and field projects? The theme would not only reflect Jay's criminal justice mission but utilize positively the disaffection of kids from the ghetto streets. If Rimbaud had been *my* idea of a deviant, the urban student's might be a child molester doing time in Matteawan, and why not? Most important, the program would counteract the anonymity and anomie of an urban commuter college by giving one hundred or so students seven professors, a remediation specialist, a field work supervisor, counselors and plenty of chicken soup.

I decided, not without misgivings, to sign on—it's hard to innovate over thirty. But it also seemed appropriate: If Sarah Lawrence had been the far out college of the fifties, we would be the pioneers of the seventies. With some handsome federal funding we created the Thematic Studies Program (TSP) over a spring and a summer. And then suddenly, in September, sitting before me in our rented quarters in Drydock Country, is the most astonishing mix of individuals ever to come to college together.

Answering the roll call are: transit patrolmen, Housing

Authority officers, firemen, corrections workers, a homicide detective, an ex-convict from Riker's Island on methadone, mothers of three from Jackson Heights, two militant and inseparable feminists, a member of the Vice Squad, Big Rosalie (red cupid bow lips, matching pumps, pastilles), college-age white ethnics from Our Lady of the Ascension, a psychiatrist's nympho daughter, undercover narcs, drop-outs dropped back in, a black female cabbie, a fingerprint analyst who skis Val d'Isere when he's not skiing Courcheval—the city in microcosm.

We barely have a language in common. At Sarah Lawrence we were separated out by subtle regional accents and varying degrees of Southampton lockjaw, but this is the United Nations without an interpreter. I launch my literature seminar in academese: "If we compare the mimesis of reality in Homer with—" This isn't going down, so I slip on my middle-class hippie cap. "Ulysses is laying this trip on them—" which doesn't sound right either, but neither do any of the other dialects spoken here. *Ici on parle . . . quoi?* Legalese: A cop refers to Camus's "Stranger" as the "alleged perpetrator" and politely asks whether his incorrect use of a comma is a felony or a misdemeanor. The only thing that sounds right is the double negative. A freshman from Riker's Island refers to Jake Barnes in *The Sun Also Rises* as "a pimp hustlin' that broad," *pace* Hemingway, who suddenly seems some effete aesthete fink along with those other Lost Generation dudes.

"Cuntegonde (sic) sure knew how to spread it around," observes another freshman in my evening seminar.

Abbie Hoffman comes to lecture on his love/hate thing with the media and there's a lot of cussin. Many students feel cheated: If there's cussin, this can't be college. A black activist from Morrisania who keeps changing his name from Clark to Kareem and back to Clark says *he* would never talk like that "in front of young ladies." Theresa G., a middle-aged file clerk from the Queens D.A.'s office, decides to leave the room when anyone uses dirty words such as frigate, intersection and misconstrue.

Our failure to find a lingua franca is symptomatic of important rifts. Soon all the exceptional individuals mobilize into warring factions and take exception to each other. I realize that the unifying theme has become confrontation, and the subject, whether we start with Kierkegaard or Kesey, is always race and things ethnic. In fact, all the racial and ethnic polarizations of the city are being played out in miniature in our classrooms.

Walter Dacey, a white detective from Mineola, works Harlem, he tells us, with his "colored partner." The term registers seismically on a black caucus at the back of the room. Never has nomenclature been so crucial. Dacey is pessimistic: "How do you give thirty or forty guys hanging out on a street corner incentive? All they want is their jug of wine—and they'd steal from their old lady to get it." Round One.

Enter Beulah Sanders. She's been invited to talk about welfare rights. Among the parasites sucking off Harlem, according to our speaker for the day, are . . . pause for emphasis—"the goddamned Jews." Round Two.

Never mind. It's the white ethnics who worry me—*everyone* dumps on the Irish, Polish and Italian kids, knuckle-whipped into mute acquiescence in the parochial schools. They're sitting here in a glaze of bursting glands and culture lag with the blacks kidney-punching 'em like it was part of their daily workout. Occasionally Miss Wisneski comes in with a counterjab—"Why don't you blacks work?" —but her queries are irrelevant intrusions, and most of the time the mode of address is "this brother here."

"Garbage strike? I never noticed. The street don't look any different."

"Canarsie? Either they open the goddam schools or we're going to burn them down."

"Jackson Heights? I don't want to cheapen your real estate."

Alfe, a natural leader, always pulls it together: "You know why we're at each other's throats? Because we're competing for the same economic places. There's only so much money at a certain level. Now I want to move in to where your father is, so you're my immediate problem."

If it's true, it's no less ominous. I begin to wonder if we aren't rehearsing for a massacre. But then came "the gun incident," clearing the air and crystallizing for many of us the sense of the program.

It's the latest head-on collision, and we've all collected into a circle like street-fight kibitzers. At the storm center, George Neville, a radical black labworker, and Bob Reedy, a towering cop with Afro and two *visible* guns. Neville is complaining loudly about Reedy, but not *to* him, which is peculiar since Reedy is, after all, right over there, in full regalia. Neville is discharging his grief through Ray, my co-professor: "This place doesn't feel like a college. Everywhere you look there's guns. It's the Wild West around here. How can we study and learn?" Neville's hands are shaking, he's so mad. Everyone shifts around uneasily; we're all aware the offender is keeping his thoughts to himself, looking off with a hurt, superior smile. He's been shot at twice, I've heard. Presumably all the hardware is intended as a deterrent. Ray is explaining this to Neville in a voice that would sweeten the incorrigibles in solitary, and the pressure is letting up a little. You see, George, it's not directed at us personally; the man's life is in danger. It's still making me nervous, though: the fact that Reedy and Neville won't acknowledge each other's presence. But it strikes me suddenly they have good reason not to: They're both black, and what's really at issue here is the rage of the black radical against his turncoat brother.

There goes Ray, seductive, steering us off *that* one: "Don't you see what you're doing to Bob, George, by griping to everyone else—tell *him* how you feel about the guns; give him a chance to let himself off the hook." And to Bob: "We understand the force requires you to be armed, but could you be less conspicuous about it? Maybe if you wore a jacket . . . ?" At some point in all this, Bob and George look at each other and smile. I look at Ray and smile, and we all laugh, from nerves and pleasure. And I realize that working through this confrontation has to do not only with George's anger and Reedy's defiance but with the terrific amount of rage floating around the place, and my own rages that I do battle with privately, and Ray's, whatever they are. . . . And somehow, along with Neville and Reedy, we've all looked at the anger and shared the difficulty of laying aside our guns, and understood that we have.

And I sense that we've reached a new plateau: We're less a school than a learning community, with the accent on community. The factions who want most dearly, *out there*, to do each other in are battling verbally *in here*, but the desire to hear one another is stronger than the desire to kill.

Kill? At Sarah Lawrence in the fifties, the on-campus homicide rate was not one of our high-priority issues. Even if we argued heatedly over whether Christ *really* loved Mary Magdalene, didn't Harold Taylor call our boyfriends by their first names? We also shared a common philosophy of education: Any idea was relevant so long as it had no gross practical adaptations (look what the Nazis did to Nietzsche). At TSP, students have the opposite vice.

No idea is relevant if it can't be fitted into one of two categories: racial and ethnic abuses, or economic inequality. I begin to worry: It's communal, it's heartwarming, it bodes well for the survival of *homo sapiens*. But is it college?

No. I thought at first—and I was collaborating in some subversive downgrading of higher education. But then the racial diatribes passed of their own accord; we were now free to begin. And I thought, yes, we had been right.

A recent study shows that experimenters pull forth the results they expect: If they brutalize rats, the rats go dumb; if they handle them "respectfully," the rats smarten up. Prior to TSP our gang had been instructed mainly in keeping invisible and accepting the original sin of their own stupidity. The positive function of the subjectivism and beefing of those early weeks was twofold: We were beating out the old negative set, the disappoint-me rat syndrome, by refusing to be disappointed, by extending our respect gratis to people who never had been listened to in school, much less with respect. Second, people who had always equated school with phoniness were taking hold of a new idea: Real feelings and college are compatible.

On my side I was letting go a lot of ideas. I had to let go my concept of who a college student is and how he should act because it was built around kids in Ithaca and New Haven strolling under the wisteria. The fact is, the student in the urban university today talks, thinks, acts and lives very differently from the soul probers of the past. Sometimes a fireman will come to class straight from having put out three fires, and a cop may come to his morning history seminar straight off the midnight-to-eight tour.

The working class student's multiple roles force him to modulate, chameleonlike, in and out of worlds difficult for the normal mind to reconcile. In fact, the personality type most likely to thrive in an urban university is the functioning schizophrenic. Leroy S. has just made a telling point about Camus's philosophy of revolt. He has also just collared a gay "round robin" in a subterranean toilet. It's Forty-second Street and Eighth Avenue, the sewer of the world, Ralph C. dubs it, and he's just been handling a homicide. Fellow stabbed on the E train. Now he's back with one of his favorite sixteenth-century French poets, Ronsard, but he's reading it in *modern*, not sixteenth-century French, which he regrets. The next day Ralph catches me before a class, his eyes rimmed pink, to help him with a nuance lost in the modern French: "Don't waste time studying and being bookish," Ronsard advises, "when you could drop dead tomorrow." It applies.

But Ralph C. is an exception at TSP because he is an old-style "good student" who would have made it to college *before* Open Admissions. Donna S. wouldn't have. Astigmatic and blurry-tongued, she has trouble marshaling the simplest concepts.

To contact our new "typical" student, I discover, we teachers have to rethink who *we* are. We have to shuck off years of training in the formal lecture style and rethink the whole experience of education.

Dumping the academic decorum starts to pay off. In comes a flurry of impressive individual projects—on prison art, policewomen, the aged, methadone maintenance, Puerto Ricans in Harlem, the Muslim shootout at a Brooklyn sporting-goods store. Not in their wildest fantasies would John Harvard or Sarah Lou have imagined that the groves of academe could accommodate such a world.

The hitch is, our pocket revolution hasn't made bourgeois culture more palatable to ghetto students. Reading now with a new double vision, I balk at the words "blackmail" and "black humor." I marvel at Hemingway's anti-Semitism, the last thing I would have noticed ten years ago but the first thing my students pick up on. Is it appropriate to ask these students to penetrate into the bourgeois world of high culture when it makes no reference to *their* heritage, when it hasn't a clue to the problems they must deal with to contrive a minimally tolerable existence? As Tony V., a black who plans to be a cop, said of Tolstoy, "What right does he have to tell us anything? He's already got what we're struggling to get." I am about to say to him, that's not the point about Tolstoy. But I don't say it. I don't say anything. Because he has touched on an incongruity so basic to this confrontation between ghetto people and high culture that I have no answer.

Neither does anyone else. All of higher education is feeling for a direction. Compounding the problem of how to educate is the fact that no one even knows how to stake off an area that can properly be called "education." The kids demand relevance and adults demand thirty credits for "life experience." B.A.'s can be earned in prison or on a cruise Ship of Schools. A mother is suing the state of California because her son graduated college but couldn't read. As if we weren't sufficiently disoriented, Open Admissions came along and blew the whole mess wide open.

TSP may not be the answer, but it's coming up with answers. One computes success in modest terms these days —like holding students in. After TSP's first year, the survival rate is stunning: Some 85 percent of its students returned to John Jay.

That smallness of scale and personalization would act as an antidote to urban anomie we already knew. We already knew about the team of counselors and remediation specialists we would need to nag and nurture everyone along. What we couldn't predict is that a small-scale egalitarian structure would generate such esprit de corps and motivation. Everyone is equally invested in the program. The students feel it is *theirs* as well as ours. And so all of us, students and teachers, surpass ourselves regularly—which beats surpassing someone else. Nor could we predict that the ambiance of support would run from student to student: The gifted ones bring the weak ones along.

So at TSP we've displaced the whole education game sidewards, onto new ground. When you've gotten yourself into a game designed for losing all round, you have to redesign the game so everyone can win. Our winning strategy is twofold. First, we've made our group process an important part of education. Everything a person does is input, even his failures; at his very worst, he is still contributing to the design. Education in our scheme is less instruction than relationship.

Our second winning strategy is to individualize standards. If someone starts at point A and progresses to point C, he is to be applauded, not flunked out because he hasn't made it to point H, where all those students at Yale started from. We've designed a winning game, we find, simply by asking people to do only what it is in their power to do. And in their own time, if necessary.

With her astigmatic eye and halting speech, Donna S. sat for months in a blur of anguish and self-doubt. Today she's talking about her thirty-page project, her thoughts clear as a glass bell. We are not as surprised as she is.

Don't Take It Personally If They Fall Asleep in Class

During my undergraduate years we lived literary characters and period sensibility. One week it was Lady Brett and Jake Barnes, the next, young Werther and his sorrows. Every Ivy campus had its Nietzschean *Ubermensch*, or Harry the Rat, since those beyond good and evil don't take precautions. And everyone played Outsider, Camus-style, or according to Colin Wilson.

Such poseurs we were—but, in our silly way, in love with books.

Some twenty years later I'm a professor, and I struggle to square my bookish past with the current vocationalism. Along with the liberal arts in general, literature has become "irrelevant," an irksome detour in the march toward a Job.

This antibook bias is not peculiar to the City University of New York, where I teach. Nationwide, the S.A.T. verbal scores have plummeted from 472 in 1958 to 429 in 1978, which indicates that kids watch television. And vocationalism prevails even at elite institutions like Columbia, where a Great Book is often just a pit stop in the race to Med School.

What is peculiar to the City University, though, is its historically new population of minority and working-class students, who gained entree to college in 1970 with Open Admissions. If for Alfred North Whitehead college was "four years of glorious irresponsibility," for these students it's a ticket to a clean desk job. If my classmates were in search of D. H. Lawrentian sensations, the new constituency wants above all "that piece of paper," the passport to a higher socioeconomic bracket.

And it's a tortuous, often awesome passage. Since the city high schools are primarily custodial, many of their graduates enter college "underprepared"—a euphemism for reading at an eighth-grade level—self-doubting and mistrustful of the figure behind the desk (whom my generation regarded as mentor and potential bedmate). Many full-time City University students, moreover, also work full time, commute long distances, tend families. So Lit 102 is less a study of "Happiness in *Candide*" than an exercise in defeating exhaustion. I've learned not to take it personally when someone falls asleep in my class.

Unlike those legendary high achievers at City College in the thirties, today's typical freshman is not buoyed up by his parents' veneration of academic excellence. Often he must "study" with TV and radio blaring, sirens screaming, the hubbub of family. For him "a room of one's own" is a rallying cry more literal than figurative—though a more realistic hope, a student once told me, is one's own reading lamp.

"Violence," a recent English Composition topic, yielded harrowing insights into the writers' nonschool hours: Almost every paper (some more intelligibly than others) told a tale of a relative shot, a friend raped, hands lopped off, eviscerations. What a vast gulf, I realized, between the bourgeois dilemmas, aspirations, even physical trappings in the books we assign, and the lives of these students. Some are as gifted and bright as any in the elite schools. But how can Gide's "gratuitous act" not seem ludicrous if your brother has been shot? And how can *Death in Venice* not seem "irrelevant" if several years of overtime, domestic crises, plus eighteen credits per semester have landed you in Metropolitan Hospital?

As one sophomore asked angrily, "What does Thomas Mann have to tell us? He's already got what we're just struggling to get." To which I have no answer. Because the faith that underpins the whole liberal arts design— man cannot live by bread alone—seems skewed among people who must still secure the bread.

But teachers cannot live on empathy alone; many of us feel ambivalent. True, we've substituted *engagement* for research, commitment to a democratic mission for lectures on stylistics. We now perform a "social" role, inculcating first-generation college students with middle-class values, enabling them to gain a foothold in the economic structure of New York City, which in turn benefits inestimably: The City University is the major source of personnel for industry and the upper echelons of the public sector. Without the university, we teachers remind ourselves, the town really would go under.

And yet our critical expertise too often goes unutilized, which produces, as all the world knows, lower back pain, demoralization and precisely the anomie we try to combat in our students. Though I should have accepted it by now, I'm still appalled that the renowned James Joyce scholar down the hall teaches remedial English.

Nor does the depressed status of our calling, far below

that of sanitation engineer, enhance morale. The professor as secular monk devoted to the life of the mind has yielded to the civil servant laboring at frozen pay in a leprous physical plant (Manhattan Community's "campus," scattered through substandard midtown buildings, is cruised by prostitutes). A student once conveyed unknowingly America's attitude toward higher education when he asked me politely: With your advantages, why don't you have a better job?

Like an embattled species in an altered environment, we're simply trying, through a range of canny stratagems, to adapt to the new terrain. My colleague Ira, the medievalist, now does research connected to social need: applying computer management techniques to the teaching of remedial English.

Others among us stretch for connections between literature and the world of urban commuter students. Bob teachs Greek drama by alluding to the modern versions in *The National Enquirer*. I jettison Baudelaire for poetry by French-speaking African and Caribbean writers. Betsy galvanizes a class with works that pit individual integrity—and financial ruin—against the pressures of a corrupt community, since economic need, for these students, is a prime mover. And Sandi, in history, makes sense of social conflict by linking the French Revolution with the Plainfield, New Jersey, race riots.

"We can't give up," she says. "Do away with the liberal arts and you get ciphers incapable of critical inquiry, automatons, not people. Somehow we've got to plant the seed. We've got to convey the faith that the twenty-five centuries preceding us matter."

Perched in an apple tree twenty years ago reading Rimbaud, it's not what I would have imagined.

Engaged to Be Separated

You may not be frivolous enough to care, but my friend Phyllis just gave a party at which the male population outnumbered the female. What's more, the males were largely unmarried, possessed gross motor control, no criminal records, a command of English, and paying jobs.

Now this event took place not on a sheep ranch but in an urban center. Over the past decade the urban center, you may have noticed, has seen a mass exodus of eligibles for Alaska, or the biker bars and other points out of the closet. But since it's considered passé to dwell on men (particularly by those who dwell *with* a man), and you want to get on with your work, you pretend indifference at these dismal demographics. You have learned to spout homilies about fish needing bicycles. You have learned to pretend it's normal to stand in a room of wall-to-wall women also pretending it's normal. You have learned to pretend it's normal to have your bosom ogled by a friend's husband.

But Phyllis was uneducable. Quiet desperation was wrecking her health when she picked up the new line coming down from shrinks: A woman should use the same creativity in her social as in her professional life; join the audacity of Cezanne to the cunning of the Desert Fox. In a time of disaster, be it war, pestilence or a skewed population, no tactic is too demeaning.

Galvanized into action, Phyllis stole the mailing list for the Ileitis and Colitis Foundation socials, then broke into the Classified department of *The New York Review*. Then hit on a less radical but more fertile maneuver: enlisting Old Boyfriends. Out of the hot seat and exempt from demands, they made eager allies and superb conduits, reaching around their lives to ferret out a forlorn Newly Single shuffling about the Operating Room; a scholar drowning in palimpsests, who could be dusted off and spruced up. . . .

As moving camouflage, Phyllis also included a few harmonious couples and, for a touch of *haimish*-familial, her son Trevor—lest anyone get the idea they were back at some mixer, circa 1954. They were, of course, only with more chins and fewer illusions, but never mind.

And *voila!* The event is launched. Visually it is sublime. A restoration of the natural order. This is how God set it up in the first place. But Phyllis is too euphoric to benefit. She freezes, open-mouthed, along with a cadre of E.R.A. activists bunched at the entrance. After years of wall-to-wall women, the behavior has to be relearned. Dazedly they skate around touching backs of chairs, trying to acclimatize to normalcy, like astronauts to weightlessness. The men, too, are disoriented by seeing so many of their own sex outside the locker room—and not sure they like it.

Alas, Phyllis's rapture soon evaporates with the Moët. The recruits may look like Apollos of Merrill Lynch, but eligibility stops right there. Too audacious and cunning for her own good, she has amassed, she realizes, a group of Ersatz Eligibles.

Most insidious, and in the widest range of shades, are

The Unavailables: Philandering Phil is a dashing sports-man with a serious limitation. It is known as a wife, ac-quired some time between Phyllis's invitation and tonight. His acquisition, he seems to feel, need not obstruct his social life—after all, a fellow should keep his hand in.

Though Phil is outrageous enough to be harmless, On-the-Fence Fred is a trickier, more tantalizing item. Fred is somewhat separated, though not yet, or something in be-tween. One might classify him Engaged to Be Separated (a category yet to be honored in the social pages of the *Times*, which lags behind changing mores.) He has one foot in the marriage, one out, depending on his wife's analysis, his wife's love life and his own fluctuating need for revenge, which usually yields to the terror that she'll get the *apartment about to go co-op*. One assumes Fred orients himself like the American tourist abroad—i.e., it's Saturday night, therefore I must be married. Since Phyllis's party is a Tuesday, he is a mere plane flight away from divorce—and happy to detail his marital messes in living color. Suspicions are first aroused when Fred is overheard saying: "Now that I'm leaving Meg the sex is so good."

Stinting Stu is divorced, technically speaking, but merely on loan from his Ex, practically speaking. She has com-plete call on him, it soon becomes clear, in the event of hamster deaths, blown fuses, or heavy snowfalls. And un-like a doctor, Stu has no one covering for him. Ex-Mrs., it is rumored, also has right of first refusal on his girl friends as potential stepmothers to her brood.

Fleeting Frank is witty, charming and much appreciated for coaxing Trevor out from under the coatrack, where he has been reading *Men In Love*. The hitch: Frank has a fiancée, sort of (Engaged to be Engaged), on indefinite leave in Somali. These ties to a place that may or may not be in Africa make him available mainly for the odd lunch. Sadly, no one here admires Frank's old-style morality smacking of needlepoint and the nineteenth century, even insinuating that Ms. Somali is more alibi than reality.

Most elusive of the Unavailables is Hedging Hank. He is rumored to have a female roommate—but since he arrives alone, the mystery remains: Does he or doesn't he? In her waning euphoria Phyllis asks. Hank's answer is unilluminating—he is not a veteran litigator for nothing. Phyllis investigates further but no one seems to know. Maybe Hank himself doesn't know. Maybe his roommate doesn't know. The enigma, Phyllis concludes, is best left to the Census Bureau.

Somewhat more available but not necessarily more eligible are:

The Aging Preppy. With his sandy tousled hair, duck-motif tie, Nantucket reds, powerful torso from racing the family's cutter (see *The Preppy Handbook* for further details), he is visually arresting but, alas, psychologically arrested. To judge by Chip's verbal repertoire, he has never gotten beyond the emotional range of Dink Stover at Yale. His Lawrenceville thirtieth reunion was "super!" not to mention "good fun"; other peak experiences are "awesome" or "outstanding." His wife is rumored to have thrown him out because twenty years of nagging failed to fatten his repertoire. "What's Chip like?" Phyllis asks his best friend. "Dunno," replies the friend, "Chip has never told me anything personal." Chip's most satisfactory tie may be to his golden retriever, snoozing under the coat-rack next to Trevor, back in the Golden Showers of *Men In Love*.

The Status Hunter is small and bald, displaying much

gilt when he laughs. It quickly becomes apparent, though, that no woman here measures up. Phyllis is out because of her address (only Seventy-first to Seventy-third between Fifth and Park, or West Sixty-seventh, please); another he rejects for her job (employed, horrors, by the public sector). The only woman who need apply is a Nordic under-thirty company president without cellulite, who looks up to her man. Such perfection he may not find in this room. (No matter, he will find it in some other room.) He leaves even earlier than

Ubiquitous Earl, the six-party-a-nighter. This Ersatz Eligible never tarries for fear of sprouting barnacles or developing a relationship. He covers so much ground, at least one half the women in any space haven't yet caught on.

The Disaster Area is totaled by impotent rage since his wife found sexual fulfillment with a Magyar. He twitches, he gnashes. Nurturing instincts kindled, Phyllis is set to play Sister of Mercy, but bourbon spiked with dope lands him comatose on her four-poster bed. Accustomed to the usual ratio, *The Whiner* is unfit for survival in this 60/40 environment. Lack of competition has made him soft and plump as a eunuch, spoiled as an Oriental vizier. He trails Phyllis around the room, whining pitiably: Where are the women?

And let us not forget *Psychobabbler,* seeking to interface with all comers, some of whom would gladly interface with him if they could only translate "interface." And finally, *The Computer Continental,* leaking the sort of Gallic charm Americans fail utterly to appreciate. Methodically he works the room, feeding into a terminal names, phone numbers, addresses—none of which he will utilize.

Look what happens when you defy the status quo, you are thinking. Better to get on with your work. Better to blink benignly at ogler husbands—or pinch them back. Better to pretend the unnatural order, though one shitty deal, is perfectly natural.

And yet, Phyllis maintains, there was a certain elation to the experience. A thrilling sense of hubris in tampering with the ratio. An artistic high in creatively engineering an environment rarely seen outside a logging camp. Getting there, Phyllis insists, was half, if not all, the fun—along with the post-mortems, which tied up phones for weeks.

A sober reassessment is nonetheless in order. If what's available is in fact *un*available—not to say unlovable—a woman may need to adjust her expectations downward. Maybe eliminate them altogether. Or she can think positive. After all, how bad could it be to hear On-the-Fence Fred describe the perfect bachelor pad he is on the verge of taking—if you only interface with him every third Tuesday?

Feminine Upkeep

I have this problem: Despite the consciousness revolution of the past five years, I still feel that I have to look beautiful. Men can look any old way: fat, lumpy, warty, too short, too hairy, hairless. I know a guy who is obsessively ugly. Women fall in love with him.

I don't want to have to look beautiful. I envy men their serviceable lint-shedding suits, unset hair, gunk-free skin, naked eyes. Who even thinks of how they look? Handsome is suspect; handsome is for movie stars.

To the world I present a respectable high-tone image, the Professor, sorting out the contradictions of contemporary sensibility, Nietzsche, the Absurd, the rhetoric of Malcolm X, Fanon. But I have this other round of trivia filling in the spaces of my existence: George Michaels for a "body 'n' sheen" hair treatment, eyebrow plucking, the boutiques, the dry cleaner—and I wonder if the feminine upkeep part of my life isn't more expressive of what I'm really secretly about, and the Professor stuff mere P.R. Let's get down to it: the nitty-gritty of feminine upkeep.

It starts in the morning. There is nothing crueler than the way a woman looks at herself in the mirror in the morning, checking out some heavy stuff—i.e., her age, her sexual rating, her situation in the world. It's the right moment for evaluations, since in many cases it's the only moment she will see her real face.

I do it, yes. After putting on my shoes I put on the mask: blusher, eye liner, mascara, lip gloss, powder. Doesn't my naked face represent me adequately?

I'm basically red-haired, and now that the copper is going to brown-gray, I'm having an identity crisis. "Color it," friends advise. But I have a thing about artifice. Even making up strikes me as funereal; that hectic flush and stained mouth remind me of a corpse. When I think of hair-coloring I see Dirk Bogarde in *Death in Venice*, the raven dye trickling down his jaw onto the pestilential sand of the Lido. . . .

So I make do with a wash and set. How many hours have I wrestled with rollers, or sat comatose under my drying cap? Three a week, that makes fifteen a month, which comes to 180 a year. Iceberg lettuce is 69 cents, the Supreme Court wants to elevate my morals, they're bombing in Cambodia, and here I am, moored to my cap and cord, ruminating about olive oil for my split ends.

As for the hair that's supposed to come off, I tend to ignore it, less from feminist principles than from lack of organization. I pluck eyebrows when I'm feeling fidgety and do a major leg defoliation before the summer, marveling at the time and mess. About underarm hair I get defensive. I say, to hell with anyone so provincial as to object to that (a lot of people, it turns out); it's plain they've never traveled in Europe.

Basic hygiene, of course, doesn't count. I'm not about to

grumble about rudimentary body etiquette in the Western world—*vive* Water Pik, dental floss, hexachlorophene, Scope and nail clippers! But fem upkeep begins where the basics leave off—we have to be ultrapurified, smooth and "dainty." After hosing down, I cream and gunk up, to achieve that silky-sheeny rubberoid surface that my favorite beauty parlor magazines tell me is consonant with femininity. Since there aren't any mikvahs in my neighborhood, I once tried douching—even though the practice of flushing out all traces of a living vagina has come up for a lot of criticism. I made an important discovery: I was dainty, but also . . . parched.

Never mind. I have a whole other life, a closet doppelgänger: my wardrobe. The trouble is it requires even more upkeep than I. In fact, I'm not sure whether it serves me or I serve it, since I toil to support and maintain it, to keep it fresh and jolly, to ensure constant turnover, seasonal renewal, storage and coordination. My shopping compulsion! I couldn't refuse a saunter through mezzanine Body Scene any more than a head could refuse chocolate-covered peanuts. No-bra bras for transparent little nothings, maxi slips for maxi dresses, midriffy tops for high-waist pants, body shirts for hip huggers, panty hose for a one-shot exposure without runs, lace bikinis for accidents. Car coats for cars, foul-weather gear for disaster areas, UFO overalls for rent strikes, kaftans and jellabas for Israel's twenty-fifth. Boots, boot trees, boot deodorant. Clogs, clippers, Ace bandages. Fox chubbies—died yellow. Yak chubbies! Rabbit Eisenhowers! Flea powder! Garment brusher! Folding wig stands! Turbans! Boas, Banlon scene-stealers, Grecian halters! Jeans with decals!

Pure fantasy, of course. My closet is a jungle only because I've never been able to throw anything away. In fact, with all my fussing, I'm still something of a mess. In the era of Separates, my top half looks like it needs an intro to the bottom half. "Your hair," my mother still says every so often, "why don't you try wetting it?" When I get emotional, Moroccan kohl travels down my cheek. And yet, over the years a generous chunk of every week has been devoted to conspiring to look gorgeous.

The trouble is I'm an upkeep dilettante, I lack a Calling. Here are some of the stations of *serious* self-beautification: three hours a week of tumbling and rope climbing at Kounovsky's or Bob Seed's; daily facial exercise; weekly massage and Scotch Hose at Arden's; blackhead extractions at Georgette Klinger's. Hair waxing, and that includes eyebrows, and pubic-hair pruning for bikini crotch shots. An alternative is electrolysis (killing the root of the hair by passing a small electric current through a fine needle). Removing breast hair takes fifteen quarter-hour sessions. You can get nail and hair transplants, semi-permanent false eyelashes. Blonde? Try eyelash dyeing. Cosmetic surgery can now correct all of nature's blunders. You might want your freckles deep-peeled off, a Doda-esque bosom for the fall, evidence of cerebration removed from your forehead and blubber removed from your gluteus maximus. Spend the afternoon in a Sauna girdle—"it works like a steam bath"—or in an Isotoner Chin Strap. Silicone injections will plump out any facial or bodily sags. Do a couple of weeks at a fat farm or beauty spa (Maine Chance in Arizona, the Greenhouse in Texas, the Golden Door in California). But we never said it wouldn't cost (a cool million), or take time (all you've got and then some).

Even an amateur like me is victimized by fem upkeep because it not only siphons off hours of time every week— it's ninnifying. Imagine a neurosurgeon pasting on eyelashes before scrubbing. We mustn't leave the house, even to go to the deli, without applying eyeliner. Is there no place, short of a POW camp, where I am entitled to look only like myself?

Upkeep doesn't stay constant; it's cumulative. The more you do to yourself, the more you *have* to do. The body may just have its own inscrutable wisdom, a balance we tamper with only to pay the dues. Leg shaving, like lawn mowing, tends to encourage bushier replenishment. Constant shaving and waxing makes hair darker. Coloring, bleaching, straightening, perming, knocks the bejezus out of hair—and you enter the condition-go-round to wheedle it all back to life. Electrolysis can create burn scars—which then have to be surgically erased. Silicone shots require round-the-clock vigilance, since the damnable stuff has a tendency to "travel" from one site to another.

Though my own facial rehab is minimal, I realized recently it is no longer optional: When I appeared one day at a curriculum meeting without blusher, everyone asked me if I was sick. That unnerved me. A rage boiled up. I thought why do I do it? Why are we compelled to self-beautify? The Visigothic self-mortification, who is it for? What for?

A man can look lined, seamy, paunchy, and still be considered attractive. He is entitled to let his life show on his face and body. Not us. Society insists we chalk out on our faces all traces of struggle, of pain, of growth, of life lived and being lived. Our bodies are . . . miraculous! Like ballerinas they will deny the pull of gravity. We are invited to deny reality altogether and model our physical selves on a few approved standardized Looks—the *Vogue* aristo, the Clairol mom, the *Oui* nipple fetishist, and so on.

The fact is, a woman's desirability in this society is still largely determined by how she looks. A man makes it on work—his desirability is determined by competence, power, money (hardly meaningful criteria in themselves, of course). But women are taken, literally, at face value. Moreover, beauty is the ticket to the good life. Until the Movement threw the whole thing into question, a woman aspired mainly to win a place in the bucket seat next to Mr. Wonderful. The million-dollar cosmetics industry promises to put her there if only she will deep cleanse, moisturize with turtle oil, and glue on some wash 'n' wear lashes.

All that may be good for my face but it does rotten things to my head. What am I saying about myself if my dominant concern is how I look? I am saying that my self-esteem depends on my physical appearance. Now there's nothing wrong with wanting to look nice. Who in her right mind would want to look like shit? There is a form of craziness— and I'm thinking of myself in certain periods of my life— that utilizes looking terrible as an act of aggression directed against oneself. Looking lousy can translate as, "I have so little regard for myself that I look this lousy." A correlate might be, "If I cared about and for myself, I would try to make myself as attractive as possible."

But what kind of attractive? I think of a very able woman I know who has never been near a beauty parlor, dispenses with makeup and wears clothes that ignore rather than defy fashion. She is an attractive woman whose sense of worth obviously has more to do with the important and demanding work she does than with Pucci or Sassoon. I personally find compelling qualities that have nothing to do with style or makeup: warmth, wit, strength, centeredness. Women are learning—and the battle is far from won— to value themselves directly and not secondhand, so to speak, through the acceptance of a man. We are learning to feel, I am an attractive person and have value not because I have won this man's approval but because of who I am and what I do, and if that happens not to be aesthetically computable, well, let the rest of the world do the accommodating. Women want the right to look any old way.

Liberation Shock

The notion that all men are oppressors, rapists or some variant thereof marked a necessary phase of the feminist revolution. But the moment has come to retire man-hating to its niche in history. It is time to view men in a calmer light, to understand how it looks from their side.

Like women, men are also boxed in by constricting roles: If she's a sex object, he's a success-object. The corporate fat cat with the chips to lay on the board can glory in such a role. But what of Joe Average, hassled by the boss, jostled by the competition, his earnings siphoned off by taxes and inflation? This put-upon fellow is nonetheless expected to take responsibility for the whole show, from sex to subsistence to finding a parking space. He is expected to play God. He must never, on pain of sissyhood, fear, falter or fail. And unlike a woman, he can't turn to his own sex for comfort and support, because he is so thoroughly conditioned to maintain a front of invulnerability and control. Of itself, this seems an unworkable agenda. But now, compounding the garden variety stresses, comes a new whammy: the women's movement.

To discover how they are absorbing the shocks of liberation, I talked to a wide spectrum of men across the country. Though an "enlightened" minority lauds feminism as the greatest "ism" to come down the pike, many more men feel fearful, angry and, above all, bewildered. Generally speaking, the bewilderment arises from the fact that if women are in transition, men are standing still. The sexes are out of sync, and communication is at an all-time low. More than ever before, men, locked in the past while women sprint toward the future, are at a loss to figure out what women want.

Even the most superficial social transactions have turned bewildering. Placed on the defensive, accused of being either macho or condescending, a man feels he can do no right. If only he knew how not to offend. He used to know how not to offend. He even used to know how to please. But these days the whole English language is a minefield, from words for the female sex (he jettisoned "gals" and "girls" long ago) to the word "manhole." And the simplest gestures of civilized life have become political dynamite: Should he walk curbside? Help on with coats? Take arms? Light cigarettes? Open? Order? Pay? Stand? Sit? Lead? Follow?

But the social hash is only the surface. Deeply troubling to men is the fact that their former helpmates suddenly view them as Oppressors dedicated to the exploitation of the female sex. Yet these men remain as they've always been: loyal, upstanding husbands and providers—which is precisely the problem.

Take Bud Byers, a thirty-eight-year-old chemist and model husband. Suddenly his wife behaves like he's Public

Enemy Number 1 encamped in their new split-level home. It started when Mary joined a local consciousness-raising group. One night she says to him: "You could walk away and leave me, so I've got to go back to school and get my B.A." Bud is flabbergasted. Leave her? *Him?* But he's loyalty itself. And he has a good job, he can provide for both of them. So far as he can tell, she's talking a foreign language; she's lost touch with reality.

Next, Mary comes home from meetings fighting mad. She refuses to cook for him. And then she won't sleep with him. "Understandably," Bud says bitterly, "considering that the group was filling her ears with catchy little slogans like 'A woman needs a man like a fish needs a bicycle' and 'Love is a victim's response to a rapist.' "

Yet Bud is above all bewildered; he's at a loss to match his self-image as loyal husband with his wife's *politicized* image of him as Man-the-Oppressor. True, he would acknowledge, historically men have raped, pillaged and oppressed—men like, say, Genghis Khan. His boss is no prince either. But why should he, Bud, take the rap for all the crimes of men ever since the first Neanderthal took his female against her will?

Other men are bewildered by the fact that they now get flogged for the very same qualities that used to win them points. Jack Henry, an Akron accountant, used to get points for his strength, ambition and take-charge style. But these days his wife Sue gripes about precisely the qualities that once attracted her. What Jack fails to realize is that the times have passed him by, that yesterday's take-charge guy is today's overbearing chauvinist hampering a wife's struggle for self-definition.

All Jack knows is he thought he had a perfectly okay marriage, when suddenly Sue starts making noises about "finding her identity." Which is fine with Jack, except he has yet to meet a real live identity. Still, he'll support her, he says (both senses, he thinks). Why shouldn't she use her education?

She turns her jewelry-making hobby into a business. The business takes off. He's so proud of his Sue. But she resents his proprietary smugness, she says. And she's changing in ways he can't understand. Change. Change all you like, he says. But just let me be me and come with you. I can't grow *and* live with you, she says. You're so domineering. You crowd me. You made it on your own, why can't you understand that I have to make it on my own too?

But Jack can't understand that Sue, long accustomed to owing whatever she's gotten to him, wants this once to owe only herself, and to make her mark independently of his "help," now seen as "controlling." And Jack feels hurt and bewildered because all he asked was to come along and, well, help.

Still other men are disoriented by a fundamental disagreement with women over the traditional contract between the sexes, which reads: He brings home the bacon, and she's there for him. Men by and large are upholding their part of the contract. Women, though, are saying, Let's rethink the whole contract. Both have their reasons: Men want to stay with the old contract because they feel it offers them an okay deal; women want to change it because they're in search of a better deal.

Women are saying to their take-charge, care-taker husbands: I can't afford the risk of relying on your goodwill for my survival. Because should you default on your goodwill, I'm up the creek.

The facts justify women's struggle toward economic self-reliance. Even though men of goodwill abound, a diamond is less and less often forever (the Census indicates that one in three marriages is slated for divorce). And a woman may suddenly wake up severed from her marriage (perhaps be-

cause her husband ran out of goodwill), without severance
pay, fifty, fat and unemployed—*and then what?* Welcome
to the new poverty class is what. (These newly poor are
Displaced Homemakers, six million strong, who cruelly
illustrate the economic plight of divorced or widowed
women who played by the old rules.)

But along with economic self-reliance, women want a
better-quality domestic life, with shared household duties
only the beginning. Highest priority would be the forging
of a new style of relationship marked by greater mutual
awareness, with the emphasis on "mutual." Always, in the
old contract, she was there for him—but in the new one he
would also be there for her.

"The trouble is, few men share what they believe to be
Utopian visions," explains Dr. Robert Brannon, author *of
The 49% Majority: The Male Sex Role*—and a bona fide
male feminist. "Men have grown up without realizing the
importance of emotional support. They have never spent
much time or energy thinking about the quality of a relationship. They focus on the quantity of cash coming in and
going out, and view home as a haven in a heartless world,
not as a setting to augment mutual awareness. So when
women start asking for these other kinds of support—for
sensitivity, responsiveness—men are caught short."

"I was so hassled by my job," says Sidney Mills, a fifty-
one-year-old salesman, "I didn't even know my family life
was in crisis." But in crisis it was—from the moment Jan,
his wife of twenty-eight years, picked up a copy of Betty
Friedan's *The Feminine Mystique.*

"You run the show, you run me, I live through you,"
Jan said one evening to Sidney. Sidney put his wife's churl-
ishness down to change of life—and put in a lot of overtime at the shop. One night he complained to a buddy
about the foul weather in his house, and the buddy advised

him, "Kick the bitch." He would keep his own counsel, Sidney decided.

Except the women in his house go on strike. No food. And he's welcome to twirl dials on the clotheswasher and bake his socks dry in the oven. They tell him he's insensitive. They tell him he's not fit to live with. Which makes him want to slam them. Because who's paying the mortgage? Yesterday, king in his own castle; today—well, he might as well face it: despised by the most important people in his life.

Then Jan announced: "Things change or I leave." Remembering that a neighbor's wife had recently deserted, Sid listened carefully. Like most men, she told him, he had to run things and control her and every situation. By perpetuating her dependency, she told him, he thrived, he felt important and alive. Even when he was home he was never "there." He didn't listen, didn't respond and wasn't accountable for what he said.

The terrible part, Sid thought, was maybe she was right. *But who wanted to hear it?* And who could understand how *he* felt? Alone, is how he felt. It would be unthinkable to say to another man: My life is coming apart. The guy wouldn't know how to handle it, he'd use it against Sid. . . .

He felt scared; the rug was being pulled out from under him. Twenty-eight years of marriage, his habits, hers, *him* —declared invalid. He felt helpless. "Respond to *her* needs," she kept repeating. But how? He'd never really thought about her needs. He thought she had everything she needed.

But mostly, he felt: It's not fair. After all, it takes two to make a "sexist household," as Jan called it. Maybe he ran her life, but *she'd let him.* And she refused to see her complicity. Why was he suddenly the heavy?

In time, Sid and Jan worked it out. Sid came to admire his wife's courage: "It takes a lot of guts to rock the boat at Jan's age." Jan, in turn, encouraged Sid's efforts to be more sensitive. Eventually he trusted her desire to redesign —not torpedo—the marriage. "At first all I could do was yell," Sid admits. "I had no experience in negotiating at a personal level; I simply wasn't trained to worry about a woman's emotional needs." But, he feels, were it not for Jan's "swift kick in the butt," they would have continued in a life he now considers deadening.

Other men, far less flexible than Sid, remain frozen in their initial response to women-on-the-move: fear. Specifically, men fear women's assault on a quarter most dear to them: their jobs. "This anxiety is difficult for women to appreciate," feels Dr. Brannon, "because until recently women have never identified themselves with work to the same extent as men—most still don't. But a man's job pretty well defines him—in the eyes of women, he suspects, as well as men—and his income and status are tightly bound to his masculinity. His job is the one thing that gives him a little platform, makes his wife look up to him. So if she enters the work world, his unique achievement is undermined."

But there's a darker, fantasy component to men's fear of women in the market place: Men are afraid that once women get a foot in the door they'll take over. (That women have only a token presence in the major corporations does little to inhibit male dread.) Cleverly playing on these fears, "Men Under Siege," an ABC television documentary, showed a successful, dynamic newscaster, Joyce Shanks, ordering around the male crew—and deftly relieving them of their masculinity. Joyce has also walked out on husband Doug, because Doug "held her back," and left him the care and raising of their child. Even more ominous, *his* career is stagnating, while hers—without Doug to "hold her back"—is booming

Though the Joyce Shankses of this country constitute a wee minority, she crystallizes men's nightmare that women will reduce them to coffee carriers, appointment stewards and mommies.

The eventuality men fear most, though, is that they will be emotionally abandoned by women. According to psychotherapist Dr. Jerry White, a specialist in men's problems, "Men need women more than women need men. And men's greatest fear is that women might declare: 'We don't need you; we can get along without you.'

"Men need women inordinately," says Dr. White, "because women are their only human connection. This stems from the fact that boys are raised by mothers—and this rapport with the opposite sex carries into adulthood." While women form nurturing ties with each other, men, despite sports or some activity-as-pretext, have only buddies. A man can't open up with a buddy, because always he has to keep up his guard and appear invincible. "Because he's cut off from his own sex," says Dr. White, "a man is overly dependent on the woman as all-purpose emotional provider. This overloads the relationship, poisoning it for both of them."

If most men fear their expendability at some dim preverbal level, their anger at the new female assertiveness is boiling away right up at the surface. Men are accustomed to exercising the absolute power of an Oriental potentate, and when women demand a more democratic arrangement, men kick and scream. Peter Wasserman, for example, hard-driving exec and man's man, is snorting mad purely because he's being asked to change the way he's lived all his married years. As he phrases it, "I did abso-

lutely what I wanted when I wanted and how I wanted."
The old contract in its purest form. Suddenly his wife puts
the squeeze on—but coming at him crabwise, not with the
frontal fury of Jan Mills. She asks him to give, just a little,
to be there, not even for her especially but for the children. Peter stiffens: He doesn't want to be "dragged into
domestic responsibilities." He wants "to keep clear." He
wants to "hedge against total commitment." He wants "to
play soccer with the boys." He wants, he wants.

Men such as Peter, says Dr. Brannon, like being king
and want more than their piece of the pie. And they feel
they can get their way by whining, by playing on a woman's ever-ready guilt. Thank goodness most women now
have the guts to say, 'It was nice for you while it lasted,
but now the game's over. Women were not put on this
earth solely to make life sweet and agreeable for men.' "

More worthy of sympathy is men's anger at an ingenious
form of psychological torture: the double bind. Men feel
they're being asked both to succeed on the job and also to
take more of the woman's role—and they see these dual demands as not only overwhelming but contradictory. The
dilemma of Baltimore accountant John Levins is typical.
The pressure at work is enormous. Then he comes home
at night and, Thwack, his wife hits him with nine other
demands: Be more domestic, relate to the kid more, be
there for me, and so on. She's placed him in a double
bind, John feels. Take more domestic responsibility—but
if he does, the job suffers. And she also expects him to be a
success. In fact, his lovability, he suspects, depends on his
success. So if he gets more involved at home, he slips on
the job—thereby losing her love. He gets the maddening
feeling she wants to sabotage him, because either way he
loses.

Still more galling, John feels that even if he *could* play
Superman, there's no payoff for him. What's he getting in

return but new bills—for her tuition and more babysitters? He doesn't have the vision to perceive that his increased investment in their homelife will yield high dividends, that a woman who feels valued beyond her function as laundress will make a better wife, and that children profit more from having an involved present father than a distracted absentee one.

It may well be, though, that women are asking men to conform to an impossible ideal, to incorporate in their personalities two contradictory sets of traits. Women want a man sensitive and nurturing—yet on the flip side, they also want him hard-driving and powerful. And it just may be that the Sensitive Bigshot is an imaginary hybrid, more female fantasy than male reality. For a tenderhearted man with an aptitude for the domestic life is most likely not the fellow who can muscle his way to the top. Conversely, Top Banana may have no aptitude whatever for intimacy and domesticity. In short, women flock to the successful man— yet they find repugnant the personality he needs if he is to succeed. As John Levins all but yelled: "She wants me to be a hotshot and earn more money, which takes total dedication to the job. And then she complains I'm driven— but that's just what it takes to make it in my business!"

Say a man goes to great pains to custom-alter his personality to please New Woman. But he then discovers that she doesn't really like the vulnerable, sensitive egalitarian, that under the glib-speak she prefers the rough, gruff guy of yesteryear—and this may just be the nastiest kicker of all.

A small but growing number of "changing men," as they like to be called, believe that the true source of men's troubles is not women, but rather the traditional male role. "Men have victimized themselves," says Dr. White, "by subscribing to the me Tarzan/you Jane syndrome. They have little human intimacy, drive themselves until they drop, live a grim narrow life—yet feel only a nameless inarticulate rage and depression." So men stand to gain immeasurably from women's efforts to loosen strangulating roles.

One giant benefit for men is simply the discovery of feelings. Sid had learned from boyhood to live as if his emotions were vacationing in the Urals. "Just think of all the men walking around with that no-affect glaze over eyes, voice and soul. You could call it 'masculinity disease,' and more men than realize are dying from it."

Women's push for equality lifts a huge burden off men by equalizing responsibility, by making women co-partners. If the car breaks down, the pipes burst, the sex stagnates and the savings run low, it's no longer *solely his fault*. Nor must he always be strong and invincible. "I don't have to play God any more," says an engineer from Long Island. "If I'm not sure, I can say so. It sure beats the old macho bluff and bluster."

Many men value the financial cushioning and freedom to maneuver afforded by a second paycheck in the family. When Jan got promoted to assistant manager, Sid was able to ease up at the office, even take extended vacations—an unimagined boon. A young social worker, thanks to his live-in girl friend's salary, was able to leave a detested job for a lower-paying but more satisfying one.

Paul Jarrett, a St. Louis architect, describes the system of mutual advancement he and his wife devised as "catapulting." Paul doubled up on domestic duties while Judy got her degree in counseling. Then, when she took a university position, the added income permitted his lifelong dream of forming his own firm. Now Judy gets home earlier so he can put in the necessary hours at his new office; but when she goes for her doctorate, Paul will again cover at home. Their one worry: Two full-time careers may prove a strain on the children—although, Paul adds proudly, Judy's a wonderful role model for their daughter.

Listening to Paul, I sensed no choked animosity toward a wife's aspirations, so prevalent among the men I'd interviewed. Far from threatening Paul, Judy's career gratifies him. Rather than fracturing their union, Judy's selfsufficiency has solidified it. I sensed, too a lack of militancy, an unwillingness to push the implications of equality all the way. In a crunch, Paul's job comes first: They might relocate for his, but not hers. Is their harmonious arrangement bought, as always, at the cost of the wife's sacrifices? Not precisely—because July and Paul see their life together in terms not of sacrifices but of gains. And if Judy places the demands of her family above dedication to career, Paul, too, keeps his marriage and children at the center of his life.

Couples who survive the inevitable collisions arising from women's struggle for self-worth seem to have in common adult strategies and caring attitudes. They understand, in one husband's words, "the importance of talking and trusting," of slogging through the knotty stretches till smoother terrain is in view. If a husband draws on reserves of patience while his wife finds her way, she, in turn, is equally generous, cheering him on as he sheds the knee-jerk reactions of the past and triple-steps into a more fluid present. Each believes that the other is worth it; if all else is in flux, their mutual commitment remains stable. They place their investment in their marriage and family above the cult of self, above the imperatives of narcissism. And this sense of partnership, in which her gain equals his, allows them to convert the shocks of change into unsuspected pleasures.

School for Ex-Wives

In *An Unmarried Woman,* Paul Mazursky's ode to male empathy, Jill Clayburgh has problems: Should she spend August in New York searching for her li'l ole self? Or should she buzz up to Vermont with Alan "Mr. Right" Bates, risking loss of autonomy?

All unmarried women should have such problems. The divorce explosion (there were 1 million divorces in 1977 and the rate is accelerating) is creating a noxious fallout, an unprecedented group of casualties with far crueler problems than Jill's. Women without degrees, jobs or "job readiness." Women isolated, demoralized, ill, suddenly impoverished—advantaged on paper, yet barely coping.

Worst off are the older women—victims of changing mores, caught playing by the rules of an obsolete game. They were Total Women. Perfect. Careerists in homemaking. Mid-game, the rules change: Marriage is no longer a lifetime engagement. "We've grown apart," Sam Buckley announces to Helen one night just shy of their thirty-second anniversary. (These are not their real names.) Two days later Sam departs. Helen has been fired from marriage. She is a walking obsolescence, tossed on the scrap heap of laid-off wives.

Theoretically, women in Helen's plight have recourse to alimony, but that's a rare thing indeed. Of the 14 percent of divorced men who are ordered to pay alimony, 7 percent comply. Of the 44 percent of fathers ordered to pay child support, fewer than half comply. Lawyers are loath to handle enforcement matters partly because—*catch*—if the women could afford a retainer, enforcement wouldn't be necessary. So let 'em work. But if they've never worked —*catch*—they can't get a job. And the job market's nether level, where they qualify to toil, is shrinking.

For those who can't afford to be delicate, there is welfare. That is precisely where many divorced women go. In 1971 the largest single group on welfare in the country was the 10.6 million women and children receiving Aid for Families with Dependent Children. And it is not only the already poor who go on AFDC. Divorce *creates* poverty. (In the sixties, when the divorce rate soared, so did the number of families on welfare.) In fact, according to a Rand Corporation report, many ex-wives are ex-affluent, and the fathers of many children on AFDC are doctors and lawyers —a new species of white-collar criminals, you might say.

Helen Buckley sits in the $80,000 house in Hartsdale wishing she didn't have to sell. But she's desperate. Buyers must smell it: Why else did one offer her $25,000? The truth is, she's late on the tax payments. The truth is, there is no food in the house, no gas in the car. "I don't think we get along so well anymore," he'd said lamely. The truth is, Helen hadn't noticed.

She has had Sam traced. He's shacked up with a young psychologist in Texas. But he's hard to reach. Helen's lawyer wants another thousand before he'll proceed. And she never saw this coming. The young psychologist must think *his wife nagged him to death.* Helen does not wish Sam well anymore.

"Get ahold of yourself," her friends tell her. "There's emergency assistance. Food stamps. Get a job," they tell her. But her credentials are charities, the PTA. . . .

Tish Sommers, firebrand head of the Older Women's Rights Committee of the National Organization for Women, has coined a term for women like Helen: Displaced Homemaker. (Tish is one herself.) It evokes the plight of war-torn refugees; it means displaced from the role of wife and, sometimes, displaced from the home as well. The D.H. slips between the cracks of existing government subsistence programs. If her children are eighteen or over, she's ineligible for AFDC. If she's not yet sixty, she's ineligible for Social Security. Having forgone the paid labor force, she's ineligible for unemployment insurance. And now, with the demise of the extended family, who is to take her in? Suddenly, with an estimated 6 million displaced homemakers in the land, divorce seems less a personal tragedy than a social disaster.

To the rescue has come the Center for Displaced Homemakers. The first was established in Oakland, California, the second in Baltimore, and there are several others around the country, including one recently opened in Buffalo. Considered a successful pilot model, the Baltimore center rehabilitates the D.H. by first building emotional readiness, then "job readiness." The women who venture into the cheery brownstone in a state of postmarital blitz, as disoriented as typesetters overtaken by computers, are desperate for work. But their self-confidence is in shreds. They feel they are "over the hill," hopeless. "The most important function of the center," says its director, Cindy Marano, "is to provide experiences for displaced homemakers which can make *them* believe that they're job-ready, and help the employer believe that too."

To this end the center offers counseling, self-evaluation programs and rap groups (yes, the term flourishes outside Manhattan). To develop job readiness it provides workshops that study the labor market and map out a realistic game plan; exercises, such as imaginary job interviews; help in finding a job; and internships—on-the-job training plus a small stipend. A D.H. can utilize the center's services, which are free, at her own pace, though generally it takes four months before she's ready to enter the labor force in fields ranging from office work to washing-machine repair. She also may do academic work at a local college—either free or at a reduced rate.

The center's graduates have become secretaries, teaching aides, clerical workers, independent cleaning contractors and carpenters; some run flower concessions, some design jewelry, some work with the elderly.

An ingenious new tool in this Operation Salvage is the "transferable skills" concept. In her newspaper column Erma Bombeck has described the Kissingeresque tactics required to stem the "humming war" in her family. As any parent knows, this kind of diplomacy is of real consequence. A homemaker already has skills in mediating, organizing, budgeting, counseling, delegating responsibility, you name it. In the job market Out There, she should be prime material for a managerial slot.

Employers, though, need to be convinced: They hesitate to gamble on women who've never held a job, fearing lack of stamina and lack of conditioning to get to the shop every morning. "But more and more," says Marie Parr, a job-training specialist at the Baltimore center, "employers are discovering that the mature woman is A-one. She can cope with crises and she offers a wealth of life experience. And she's a good investment—even if she remarried she'd want to stay on because she's excited by making her own way. Female employers particularly are committed to hiring a displaced homemaker."

Along with savvy strategies to ease the shell-shocked D.H. into first-time self-sufficiency, there is an intangible curative offered at the center: supportiveness, the empathetic "I've been there" attitude of the staff, most of them former displaced homemakers. The new refugee has visible proof that even over the hill, it's not all over. Says workshop coordinator Barbara Turner, "I love working with women coming out of trauma—it's holy. It's like watching a rebirth."

A Catholic who left her husband because "emotionally, he'd left me years before," Barbara survived the trauma of suddenly finding herself the sole support of five kids. (She is now working on a master's in community development at Johns Hopkins.) When she sees the typical fifty-two-year-old come into the center, Barbara says, it strikes fear in her heart. "She's barely finished eighth grade, she has high blood pressure, varicose veins, gynecological problems, less stamina than a young worker would have."

Another staffer, Angela Carter (not her real name), once went to the bottom—like Barbara, like most of the displaced homemakers at the center. But she sees the women as flowers born of crisis, just like the flowering cactus she brought a friend who had OD'ed on Elavil. When at rare moments she thinks of the past, she sometimes thinks it was the dust episode that caused the breakup. Not her husband's drinking, not his threats, not his verbal abuse. She had spent the day cleaning. When her husband came home, he put on his white military gloves to test for dust on the transom. Angela took kids, dog, cat and $200 set aside from an unpaid meat bill, and left. She found a job, got phased out, applied with three hundred applicants for another job. "It was one rejection after another." Her married friends looked the other way: "I was a living reproach; I held a mirror to their own marriages. I was in such terrible shape, I kept half the women in the League of Women Voters married."

The center was a lifeline. "I joined it as soon as it opened—two years after I left my marriage. At that time I'd been out of work for a year, and I was really desperate." The center made her an intern in public relations; her ex-husband started sending $500 a month for the children—and then came the flowering. As a result of the self-evaluation program, she decided she really wanted to go back to art school and start a graphic-arts business. Everyone has the fantasy: "If I could do what I've always wanted"—and then stops striving, battened down by the status quo. But when all the moorings have been cut, there's a heady freedom. Angela turned down a $14,000-a-year job to take an art scholarship to the Maryland Institute. It was up to her to make the rules in *terra nova*.

Diana McLaughlin, fifty-eight, has the boundless gaiety of someone who has lost it all. Paul Mazursky could do worse than make his next movie about her. She even has gorgeous gray-blue eyes. "No one can take anything from you if you don't have anything," Diana says, flashing an electric smile. Suburban ex-wife of an affluent officer in the merchant marine, she was suddenly left, after thirty-four years of marriage, with a concave ego and a history of volunteer work. Awesome, the comfortable matrons this happens to, their lives like tidy flower beds. "After an accident, I was lying in the hospital in traction with a cracked hip. I had no hospitalization. I knew there was only one way I could go—up. I took two suitcases and my body and went to my daughter in Atlanta. 'Mother,' she told me, 'you can do anything.' She got me a ticket to Baltimore and put me on the plane."

A stint in the center's training department under a

stipend, and Diana became a small-business coordinator, helping put displaced homemakers in their own businesses. "If I could have found the center sooner—ten people in a room saying, 'Yes, I've been through the same thing'—I would have been two years farther along. You need a place like this to sit down and assess, say 'I can do that! I've already done that!' And you can go at your own pace. Most women come into this place feeling guilty, feeling *I screwed up*. Well, you've simply got to get rid of that.

"Hot dog!" Diana exclaims into the phone at an invitation to a management conference. To me: "It's wonderful to be a woman at this age in this world. My children admire me. My twenty-year-old son saw an article on me and said, 'Mom, I didn't know you did all these neat things.' "

Compared with her previous situation, Diana's salary is modest. But it's possible to live on it in Baltimore. "I don't care about affluence," she says. "I had it—my values have changed. I enjoy what I do with *my* money more than what I did with all my husband's. I spent over half my life with him. I care about him as a good friend. At first I was hurt and angry, but I couldn't live with anger. I *choose* not to live with anger.

"Working here, well, you become a living proof to the others that the thing can be done. When you're in the pits you can't see that you're going to make it; you can't see the stages of the recovery. I didn't know it was okay to be angry and cry and be crazy. No one told me that. Look, you have to have a great will to survive, and survive on your own terms. I'm not a pretender. I feel great. I love to get up in the morning and go to work. At fifty-eight I'm just finding myself. I'm not ready for love or intimacy yet. Maybe, yes, in six months—but right now my life is so filled."

Helen Buckley's story could finish this way.

Splitting the Kids

The jingly tinseled specter of it hung just a few days ahead of them, the annual psychic bombardment that every lonely person most feared and dreaded, from the first sign of turkey sales on through the incessant clanging of carols to the last bleary notes of Guy Lombardo playing "Auld Lang Syne"; the trinity of public trials called Thanksgiving, Christmas, and New Year's.

—DAN WAKEFIELD, *Starting Over*

The holiday casualties to whom Wakefield was referring are the divorced without children. But what of those with children? Our holiday problem is not so unrelentingly, grisly. Yet neither is it so wonderfully simple. In fact, the highs and lows inherent in our situation make the jolly season all the more taxing.

If you're with the kids, you feel blessed. But without them your "public trial" is crueler than if you were always solo. If you also happen to be a member of a minority religion, and not sufficiently religious to counterattack with minority rituals—stand by for psychic bombardment.

On the upbeat side, the children justify Christmas. They inoculate one against the crasser features of the season, like Zabar's and Bloomingdale's. You may even vicariously enjoy Christmas through your child's love of its visuals, its poetry, its consumerism.

Then, too, Christmas delimits giving. Without it, you might feel impelled to give the year 'round. To my daughter, Maud, then, goes the Snoopy watch that I will eventually appropriate, and to my son, Neilson, goes the duffel that Maud will eventually appropriate, provoking a border skirmish which escalates into a major incident, resolved by Mother, who thereby qualifies for the Nobel Peace Prize— and all is well in the best of all possible single-parent households.

There is, however, a Catch-25. Tucked into your Separation Agreement is a spoilsport item that decrees alternating, with your ex-spouse, custody of the kids over holidays. If the kids have already taken you through public trial Number 1, i.e., Thanksgiving, then you must surrender them over the crucial 24th and 25th. This directive excites certain base trains of thought, such as: Why be so punctilious about holiday custody when said ex-spouse fails to comply with far more crucial items?

You dismiss such legalisms as unbefitting the spirit of the season.

A second base thought assails you: You feel . . . cheated. The kids owe you. After all, you've listened to hours of "Snappy Answers to Stupid Questions" from him, and hours of "Three Blind Mice" on the violin from her.

Have the ingrates never heard of quid pro quo? Christmas in exchange for snappy violins?

But the dears are already envisioning Christmas with Daddy: a Norman Rockwell white-on-white 3-D extravaganza including midnight mass, caroling in Louisburg Square, genteel pewter and family tree ornaments in a part of the nation where Christmas—and Norman Rockwell—are embraced without ambivalence.

So where does all this leave the deserted parent? I for one rule out seeking asylum at my folks' hearth in Roslyn, since they celebrate yule by leaving it somewhere north of the Florida Keys. I therefore find myself among the Christmas Strays. Curiously, though, I feel *superior* to Christmas Strays—or at least in a special subcategory. After all, I'm a titular head of household and never mind that not a creature will be stirring tomorrow morn but the head of household plus your odd roach. Am I not a mother of two? And therefore entitled? A bona fide citizen of Christmas? (Unlike the singles disco-ing into the wee hours unencumbered by wee ones.)

But such sentiments of superiority tend to brown out well before the 24th. Guiltily, I've worked on the kids. "Will you call Mom on Christmas day? You can reverse the charges."

"Of course, Mom. But we might forget. We'll be busy opening presents."

Hating myself for putting a crimp in their childhood, I push on: "What do you all do with Daddy and his new missus on Christmas?"

"Oh, Mom, don't call her that. She's perfectly nice."

If I knew her, I would undoubtedly concur. It's just that I don't concur with her four children's manners, which mine import every other weekend.

"Anyway, Mom, you shouldn't pry," instructs nine-year-old Maud, who reads heavily in psychology. "Dad never asks what *you* do on Thanksgiving." Neilson, who is nudging adolescence and has a fine grasp of adult ambivalence, decides that a game of Mad Libs needs him more than this conversation.

I fortify myself with a memory of last Christmas day, when my ex-husband's sister—and my dear friend—phoned from Boston. "God, have I got a houseful. I don't know how much longer I can take this. *Six* kids. The cat threw up. I'm going to need a month's vacation to recover."

The memory fails to fortify. The solution lies, no doubt, as many a Stray well knows, in a Great Escape—preferably one orchestrated by the Matterhorn Club, a fish-and-hunt organization dedicated to the proposition that the single life is well worth living, particularly if unexamined. The words "Banff" and "Canada" light up my brain. Yes, Christmas in Banff is the ticket, and never mind that I haven't skied in years and that it's 30 degrees below. As a deserted parent, I'm entitled. And the life-threatening climate and sheer danger will freeze out morbid thoughts.

But I have forgotten Catch-31. The kids check back in for New Year's, clamoring for action. If I shell out for Banff, I'm limp in the wallet come the 31st. Do I indulge myself? Or do I indulge my kids? A dilemma, as all single parents know, without a solution, since either way you go you feel either guilty or deprived.

Backed into a corner, I conjure up creative solutions: Clone the kids. Come the 25th, mom and pop can each make off with a pair.

Or: He takes one child, I take the other. Haven't they been fighting all year anyway? I quickly strike this one. Even after a solid year of border-sniping and no cease-fire in view, they will brook no separation—especially over Christmas.

A third solution: Go contemporary. Cadge an invitation

to go to Boston with them. After all, single co-parents should break with stuffy tradition and resist all temptations to petty-mindedness. And the extended family is the wave of the future.

A fourth: Advertise for a guy whose separation agreement gives him Christmas custody of his kids, so I can spend the holidays with them.

Better yet: Pray, just pray some solon of the eighties will honorably discharge from the holidays all but nuclear families—or institute a two-day Christmas.

Adrift in Coupleland

She wants to join A.A., Phyllis tells me. But why, I ask. One vermouth on the rocks and she falls asleep.

But if she belonged to A.A., Phyllis explains, she'd have a community. A network to break her falls. Easy-over gregariousness, instead of her actual social life: three weeks lead time to plan a dinner party during which she's too dithery to play with her guests. She could seek asylum in a substitute family. In life's black holes they'd be *there*.

That I understand. I, too, break out periodically in nostalgia for community. Without in any way idealizing my former life as a couple, I'd still say the two of us formed a self-sufficient community, a microcosm containing the primary emotions plus off-shades.

We-as-couple also had an external community—or, rather, a New York social life. Transportable, even-numbered, color-coordinated, we herded together with other inevitable couples. Though this was not in the truest sense of the word a community, I was too absorbed keeping house in the microcosm to notice.

But I hadn't foreseen at all what would happen when we uncoupled: I forfeited not only the microcosm—but my passport to the country of two-by-two. How often I'd read about this sorry business. Ironically, I'd even written about it myself.

But knowing history is no warranty, apparently, against repeating its mistakes. I discovered, as if for the first time, that unless she's a superstar, odd woman out does not a neat packet make, especially for hosts fixated on sexual symmetry. She's as functional as an iguana in the bathtub.

Some friends chose sides, others toughed it out with both of us, contriving staggered arrivals at parties, not always fail-safe, and then what? Eventually my erstwhile social life too often resembled bombed-out Frankfurt.

All this is more on the order of sober assessment, by the way, than self-pity. I'm uncomfortably aware, though, that my *nostalgie du couple,* as the French label it, is not only reactionary but impolitic. "I perceive you as man-oriented," says Wanda with restrained horror. Yesterday's norm, today's heresy.

Well, it may be impolitic, but it's mine. And the truth of many more women than some doctrinaire feminists would like to imagine. (Why is it all right, by the way, for a man to be woman-oriented?) Few women take their solo act on the road with the same joyous affirmation as Gretchen Cryer—they're far more partial to the extended stopover with supporting cast.

But about that supporting cast. Certainly it's impractical —and counterproductive—to live as if couple-community were behind the next bush: It may supervene, and then again it may not. In fact, Wanda, who is separated, views her sojourn in couple-land as an exceptional period rather than the norm.

I'm untempted by psycho-fascism, like *est*; or the spiritual supermarket that beckons to floaters "between affiliations," as the sociologues call it; or the dry consolations of print collecting or talking marmosets. So I look around and ask, "What else?"

Theoretically, one ought to find a form of community in work, in the various occupational villages of the city. If nothing else, the team busyness distracts from any human warmth deficiencies at home.

Certainly my friends in publishing, that Perrier-and-pajama party with books, find a functional community—if not a compassionate one. Slip, my dear, and the ranks close over, not under you. And the office, says a friend, wants the public person, not the private mess: When once, just once, he revealed his marital disarray to a colleague, he was given the slow freeze.

During the period I taught in a trial program floated by my university, a glow of collegiality (rare in New York colleges, which tend to be subway stops), warmed me around the edges. But by inclination, I'm also a writer, a trade requiring solitary confinement. For hours I live with my head in a tree of talking birds; at others I have more going with my humidifier, exquisitely attuned to my nasal membranes, than with New York's other typewriter anchorites.

But there are, of course, friends: old friends who can do no wrong, and when they do, one looks the other way; a geniuslike person to whom I expose early drafts. Disparate geographically and temperamentally (convened in the same room, they might draw blood), my friends don't, however, form a horizontal community.

Nor is New York life, with its stimulus overload, particularly hospitable to friendship: It may seem more cost-efficient, at times, to neglect it. Several of my women friends are invested heavily in marriage and family, so our contacts are necessarily peripheral. But in her life, insists Wanda, women stand center stage.

I ask myself, "Why wouldn't a group of women be my community?" I recently went to an all-woman dinner party given by Wanda. I ate and I smiled and got high on the high-flying wit. Only I felt chilly, emotionally remote, as if watching through thermopane. Was this too cerebral for my base nature? Am I unable to touch down among people I don't touch?

Or was it the competitiveness? A projection of my own, maybe? Or was it outside me, too, that old tilting for men now transferred to ideas. But I knew that every woman there had been professionally generous to Wanda—and she to them. And I knew, like them, that in work it's with men, not women, we compete. And I concluded only that this was Wanda's community, but not mine, and that Sisterhood-in-the-abstract eluded me.

A coed group of equally clever New Yorkers once formed a "commune," or "extended family," in the country. Most of us armchair "communards" were, romantically speaking, "between affiliations." The one-liners at breakfast were taxing, the food fights unbecoming to adults and the ambiance was more brittle than gentle.

What may have killed us, in fact, was ineptness at peacemaking: Lovers peacemake in bed, but the communards never found alternative forums. At its best, though, we came close to something marvelous: a clannish loyalty, a familial bonhomie that I've never encountered outside blood ties or marriage.

Before that were other communes, other communities:

a Quaker co-op in Georgia, where junior year summer I picked okra and prayed in a circle; the dorm in college, where we ate up the night in metaphysical talk; ballet, claiming me like a religion.

My old neighborhood in Queens, where we roared down the block on roller skates in the fragrant May dusk or clustered on stoops discussing sin, tiny auburn ants circling our black patent-leather Mary Janes, and where anyone ailing got nonpareils from the block busybody.

And before that, back a generation, the street life of the old ethnic neighborhoods, Cypress Avenue and 138th Street, a cornucopia of games—stoop ball, potsy, puss-in-the-corner, checkers, jacks—my grandmother and my grandmother's friends, elbows on cushion, watching from windows. How populous, how clamorous, how enfolding were those ready-made communities of the past!

Today, I suspect, community starts in oneself.

Single Mouse,
Married Mouse

When Phyllis and friend sailed into the party the other night, they beamed out that excluding radiance of the "coupled." Was Phyllis about to enter the other culture? I wondered, feeling panicky, bereft, left behind.

Once again I was struck by the co-existence in this city of two communities as distinct as two ethnic groups: marrieds and singles. Between these two cultures festers no enmity, like between Hassidics and Blacks. If occasionally they interact, as when a couple is catapulted to singledom, or when a married male marauds on single turf, mainly they just ignore each other, like the moose and the capybara browsing side by side in the Central Park Zoo.

Marrieds and singles take so little notice of each other because they have unrelated goals: Marrieds want to get on with the business of living; singles have put living on hold while they hunt for someone to do it with. If the essence of the married condition is self-sufficiency, that of the single condition, despite the brave facade, is rampant round-the-clock need.

Understandably your average single is very nervous. Lean, dyspeptic and ever in motion, he is continuously—even at the sleep-disorders clinic—in search of his ideal mate. According to George Gilder, though, he is likely to die, a victim of insecurity and nervousness, before even sighting this ideal (which the male envisions as "a twenty-seven-year-old investment banker who is dynamite in bed," and which the female envisions as someone with treatable character disorders and no criminal record).

When not comatose with contentment, marrieds have a more legato style. They move slowly, because encumbered by progeny, and in even numbers. Married hostesses in particular have a fixation on even numbers and superstitiously regard odd ones, especially when female, as Herpes Mary. Marrieds also tend to move upward because, undivorced, they've kept their capital from lawyers and other predators.

Singles and marrieds differ not only in style but in all their concerns, attitudes and rituals. Take the holidays. Come November, a married gets aggravated—but a single turns suicidal. While a married awakens at 4:00 A.M. wondering how to baste the bird, a single is basting in sweat, wondering if someone's "strays" list will rescue him from Turkey Roll with all the nitrites at Roy Rogers.

And consider vacations. For the single a vacation is just a more strenuous form of work, the Action, like a carrot, always dangling before his nose. Picture any ski resort. Come sundown the marrieds are all snug in their condos, stirring fragrant stews. But for the single, a hard day on the lift lines is merely a prelude to hitting every hot tub, canvassing the bars, and flinging his charley-horsed shanks around some disco. That papoose riding down the mountain in a sled the next day? A single, *hors de combat.*

When a married thinks Caribbean, he conjures halcyon solitude. But just mention solitude to a single and he gets twitchy. To avoid it he would take a share in the leper colony around the cove.

For a wife, summer is shopping season. For a female single, it is high-anxiety season, because a cyclical indicator of the progress—or more likely lack of progress—she has made in her quest. She takes a tally: Her support group has married away, making her feel like a remnant. Astonishingly, they cease to acknowledge her, forgetting that not long ago they too were D.P.'s, that Long Island could have been Ellis Island.

She takes a share in a beach house. The results are not happy. True, in kindergarten nice children shared. But over thirty now, the children are too old to share—and also to recycle themselves, measurably slacker than last season, around the South Fork.

Even this fabled resort is rigidly segregated into single and married enclaves, the only crossover occurring when a husband jogs ten miles under the noonday sun to the singles seraglio, where women sprawl oiled and topless. But potential violence lurks in the dunes: Home-owning marrieds would like to drop off the nearest pier, with lead in their wet suits, all fun-loving single groupers.

The two cultures also differ on the subject of food. Eating is the married's primary sensual outlet. But the single, who seldom sits down to a home-cooked dinner—or even dines sitting down—is far less concerned with what he's eating than whom he's eating with.

Scarcely conscious of what he ingests, the single is subject, studies reveal, to bizarre disorders specific to his condition. Some singles, for example, suffer from prickly nape and delusions of Third World conspiracy from an unbroken diet of Chinese Take-Out. One single reportedly developed kwashiorkor-like symptoms and permanent aftertaste of brine from living on Delicatessen alone. The most frequent disorder, stemming from the common singles practice of eating standing up, is green cud and whinnying.

Some single eating styles are downright lethal. An unmarried woman heavily into self-improvement read that the Governor's bride listens to French tapes while taking a shower. Inspired, she attempted to practice her French "r" while supping—and chanting and tap-dancing —and ended up in St. Luke's with Take-Out lodged in her windpipe.

Though eating is supposedly a prelude to the evening's main fare, the sexual hyperactivity of singles is a myth hatched in the fevered brains of marrieds. The sad truth is many a single embraces the New Chastity rather than risk the new microbes—*because if he gets sick who will take care of him?* And you can't rely on appearances. One carrier, it is whispered, was a Young President and civic leader with tastes more democratic than his politics.

As if such dues weren't damper enough, single sex is dependent upon real estate. July and August, for instance, are lost to love, thanks to beach-house walls. And by Sunday 2:00 A.M., the city single is mainly in a froth over the cab fare from Soho to Park West Village.

The only serious singles action occurs in the I. M. Pei buildings in Kips Bay, where transportation problems are nonexistent. When a man feels amorous, I hear, he just strolls into the hall in his most casual attire; if he has run through his floor, he rides the elevator. Of course the place is a breeding ground for crimes of passion, not to say new microbes, but single life is at best dicey.

In fact, it scars some singles permanently—even if, like

Phyllis, they escape to the other culture. Engaged now, she still *acts* single—i.e., every night she still pastes on false eyelashes, puts her best foot forward, and chain-smokes while relating in 3-D her complete sexual history. Even more ominous, at the sleep-disorders clinic she mouths the words "asparagus beach."

Watch What He Does,
Not What He Says

A seventeenth-century French maxim has it that *plus ça change plus c'est la meme chose:* the more things change the more they stay the same. This could apply to the dating scene, which I reentered last year with some trepidation, along with 1.1 million Americans who divorced in 1977, not to mention those millions merely separated or newly disentangled from longstanding affairs.

The same old stuff? Even after the Women's Movement has toppled our obsolete codes of behavior? The trouble is, it hasn't. I discovered all too painfully that the *language* men use has changed. In their dealings with women, men now deploy the new enlightened rhetoric of liberation. But their attitudes and behavior are still sunk in the prehistoric bogs of the fifties. Worse, a lot of new talk is camouflage for old abuse.

I like assertive women, men say. Yet women friends in the field report assorted atrocities if they try to make the first move. When Toby invited a man to the theater, he said he'd have to check his calendar. The next day she received a no-thank-you call from his secretary.

The old "dinner transaction" was grotesque, but at least everyone understood it: He pays, she puts out. Now, of course, women are equals, not harlots. "Let's take liberation seriously," men say, "and split the bill for dinner."

In principle, this is excellent. But most over-thirty-five men toil in more lucrative professions than women in that age group, or are higher up the corporate ladder. (We were raised—remember?—to believe men make the primary, women the secondary income.) So given the unfortunate reality of unequal incomes, what's so egalitarian about going 50/50?

Then, too, men are freaky about money—it's symbolic of sexiness, power, status, *control*. What used to be a pleasant meal shared by two consenting adults is now a minefield of problems. On one occasion when I offered to split the tab, my co-diner got defensive, as if I were questioning his earning power—and virility. He was also alarmed that I was thereby stating, a priori, that we were to be just friends, because paying still entitled him (old morality) to sex. Though you'd never get them to admit it, in their gut many men still feel that picking up the tab means calling the shots and maintaining control —the position they're comfortable with.

But since everyone's coming from a different place, as they say in Marin County, it's hard to know with whom you're dealing. Before even touching the hors d'oeuvres we need to exchange position papers. My friend Joan went out with a shrink who was so fair-minded he wanted to split the check according to a percentage based on their respective incomes. To make it all easier he'd brought a calculator. A less fair-minded friend, to my amazement, asked me to pick up the after-dinner tip and cab fare after he'd been my guest at the ballet.

In the past, strangely enough, though men picked up the bill, women reciprocated—by cooking dinner one evening or buying theater tickets. No one kept track of who was spending what on whom, and who cared? It was assumed that reciprocating had its own pleasures. In fact, one didn't reflexively equate giving with being "taken."

After dinner isn't any easier. Here again, what men *say* doesn't reflect stubborn attitudes fathoms deep from the surface. "I like a woman who's up front about sex and doesn't play obsolete games by holding out until X number of dates." But how does this man *behave?* (Says my wise friend Phyllis, "I never pay attention to what men say, only to what they do.")

What are the consequences, for a woman, of sexual candor? "As soon as I slept with him, and it was soon," a friend says, "his interest waned. You know, long silences between dates, inattentiveness." Could it be that underneath the rhetoric a man still considers a woman "cheap" if she doesn't withhold and play the game? Could it be that the rotten old conquest mentality—it's valuable if it's hard to get—is still alive and well?

But women today are damned if they do and damned if they don't. We're practically coerced into instant sex by the prevailing sentiment that bedding down is how you get acquainted—and get second-class treatment for our spontaneity. But if we decline, what's to keep a guy around? For him it's a seller's market—there are half a million more women than men in New York. And there aren't many suitors in the environs who, like Henry James's Caspar Goodwood, would pay court for five years!

I have a lurid imagination, you say. I'm making it sound like a jungle Out There. Well, gentlemen, check around. Ask your friendly divorced woman next door. Ask any woman. She might tell you about a lack of civility between men and women. A lack of sexual etiquette. Particularly in the area of endings.

If every love affair has a beginning, it necessarily has an ending, and we don't need Descartes to perceive the logic of this axiom. All too often, though, an affair is proceeding nicely when . . . shazam! It's the magical disappearance act.

I haven't heard from X in a couple of weeks. Sepulchral silence. Could he be lying in Intensive Care somewhere while I'm thinking unkind thoughts? Before checking the hospitals I call his home. This was a mistake, I decide, since my friend and lover on the other end has not been hit by a flowerpot and moreover sounds less warm than the cold-cuts man at Daitch and has pressing business.

The Houdini syndrome is widespread, to judge by informal interviews with friends. If you were to question a man about it, he might say: "We're each our own person. I'm not responsible for her, she's not responsible for me." This reasonableness is really a fence for abuse. If someone wants to end an affair, well and good. But Houdini conveniently forgets one existed to end. And punctuation, among animals blessed with speech, is obligatory.

Phyllis the wise once asked a drop-out boyfriend to explain his modus operandi. Why didn't he at least give a call, she asked. "I wasn't ready to get involved," he answered. "I just wanted to be alone. And I thought you'd be mad."

The odd thing about this Houdini—he's an outspoken E.R.A. defender—is that he's superpunctilious in his courtesies toward men and colleagues. And if asked, he'd invoke the new slogan for man/woman relations: *Lovers are, above all, friends.*

As for me, I'll take a man who talks like a swine. There's a better chance that underneath he's a pussycat.

Without Consolations

The contrast resonates with a cruel irony. On March 10, 1980, Dr. Herman Tarnower plans to have dinner with current girl friend Lynne Tryforos. Around 1:00 P.M. he returns home from the Scarsdale Medical Group to see to the wine. On March 10, 1980, Jean Harris, his companion of fourteen years, entertains ideas of a different order. She writes a will, scrawls several "suicide notes," then drives five hours through rotten weather—to end a life.

Whose is not clear. Prosecutor George Bolen maintained that Harris shot Tarnower four times in a jealous rage over his affair with her younger rival. Defense lawyer Joel Aurnou maintained that Tarnower was killed in a "tragic accident" when he tried to prevent Harris, suicidally depressed over pressures at work, from shooting herself. In his camp Bolen had plausibility, and the notorious "Scarsdale Letter," torpedoing Harris's claim that she viewed her rival with equanimity. Feisty Aurnou retaliated with a host of forensic experts, who went on interminably about perforations of the flesh and offered rebuttals to all the points scored by Bolen. But Aurnou had a more redoubtable weapon: impassioned female identification with the accused.

Without impugning the American legal system, let me nonetheless say that the whole business is a bit of a circus, and I have no great faith that any definitive picture of the truth will emerge. I wonder if both sides aren't right: Jealous rage and suicidal feelings are not incompatible; Harris could have set out for Purchase, New York, with one motive, then segued into another. She may have intended only that the doctor dissuade her from her own bullets. No stranger to self-deception, Harris herself may no longer know what she intended—if ever she knew in the first place.

But then I am less interested finally in the central question of Jean Harris's intentions than in all the side issues. I am interested in what drove her to this act which, whatever else, was also a suicide. I am interested in why women identify so powerfully with Harris—thereby conferring on a sordid *crime passionnel* the status of media event. In Jean Harris women see themselves, and the woman they fear becoming, fight not to become, just missed becoming—feel, "There but for the grace of God go I." They read her story as a cautionary tale: For fourteen years a man and a woman keep company outside traditional structures, and he ends up with money, power and love. And she? Play it like Jean and you end up crazy, in the slammer or dead.

No one would have noticed, of course, if the man and the woman were two obscure *schleppers*. Herman Tarnower was not only the noted cardiologist and author of *The Complete Scarsdale Medical Diet*, he had symbolic credentials as well. In a culture that worships slimness he was the Guru of Lean—and for women perhaps the ultimate authority figure. Before her fall, as headmistress of the tony Madeira School, Harris was the ultimate in respectability. While the general public voyeuristically enjoys the contradiction between the outer and secret Harris—behind the starchy facade lay twisted passions—women perceive a more threatening dimension: Harris's considerable professional achievements could not save her, as they so often do men, from emotional mayhem.

Her age strikes an anxious chord in women's hearts. While the sexual vitality of sixty-nine-year-old Tarnower would be found admirable, almost mythic, an avid middle-aged woman is considered slightly grotesque. In popular fantasy, Harris at fifty-six should have been more concerned with losing her teeth than losing her lover. As a spurned middle-aged woman she reminds women of their own age-related vulnerability. Her example suggests that continuing desire will be greeted with the "jeers" she alludes to in the "Letter"—as if the sexually vital woman of middle years were on a par with some village freak. (With her porcelain features, blue eyes, celestial smile and intense manner, Jean Harris, for the record, is mesmerizingly lovely. Despite her travails and the fact that some days she resembles Ophelia among the lilies—dressed by Chanel.)

But the case goes beyond personalities; it raises larger, controversial issues—and reduces dinner parties in Scarsdale, I hear, to shouting matches between the sexes. In a sense, along with Jean Harris, Tarnower's life style is on trial. By all accounts an excellent doctor, he was devoted, with the tunnel vision peculiar to lifelong bachelors, to his own pleasures: food, wine, travel, expensive forms of hunting—and "thoroughbred women," in *Time*'s phrase. His was a life of serial loves—with overlap—Jean Harris being the next-to-last. In the public fantasy Tarnower personifies a hedonistic, dues-free existence exempt from long-term commitment, responsibility and that aging face across the breakfast table. Exempt from pain: Since he didn't really need or care about anyone, as Harris maintains, he was invulnerable. Exempt from reality: Unmarried, he told Harris, he would never have to know about her mother's nursing home. To many men Tarnower is a folk hero of the narcissistic age, the guy who could—well, almost—get away with it. Even the rabbi who presided at Tarnower's funeral praised his "desire for personal independence," comparing it, with dubious taste, to Einstein's.

Women do not share this admiration, as the defense lawyer well knows. Women feel the alleged murderer is equally a victim—not of bullets, but of antihuman, degrading treatment, of the venerable male practice of enjoying a woman during her "prime," then trading her in for a new model. The housewives who commute four hours to watch this real-life soap see a woman who put in fourteen years of devotion—rewarded in every arena but love with at least a pension and a gold watch—only to be "discarded like garbage."

Of course one had come to expect almost anything in the age of Free to Be You and Me, when men and women have fewer rational claims on each other's loyalty than ever before. But along comes an educated woman of substance who snaps. Who gets crazy. And it is a curious thing, but she is not alone in the craziness. One can dismiss as fringe loonies the women writing in, "The bastard got what he deserved." But what is one to make of all the tranquil sane women who applaud Harris?

The killing was cathartic; with Harris's .32 they vicariously gunned down their own little traitor. But there's something more: While no one would seriously maintain that a man who displeases ought to be shot through the head, neither is one happy seeing him walk away scot-free from despicable behavior. The uneasy gratification women feel at Harris's act is really nostalgia for a sense of moral obligation—which may well reflect some permanent human need. In sympathizing with Harris one is not condoning murder, but rather affirming the idea that people *are* responsible to one another, that a human being is not an invitation to plunder, that a major reform in sexual manners is in order.

For all her seeming universality, though, Jean Harris is very much the product of a past—and fading—generation. She must have absorbed the traditional values of marriage and family unconsciously, like silt seeping into the soul. She lived those values for a time, marrying an appropriate man, settling in Grosse Pointe Farms, raising two sons. A divorce later, she swung into an independent updated life, gutsily raised the boys without much money, became a school administrator, then the mistress of Tarnower—ardent, successful and, like her, socially ambitious.

But in some bottom layer she wasn't the modern self-reliant woman she appeared; later she would lack the resources, toughness and coolness essential to that role. Harris had the trappings of independence—but overlaying a dangerous residue from the past. Like the inability to make work the sustaining center it must be if you plan to go it alone. Like the tendency to place not work but a man—*one* man—at the center of her life.

She had "values from another era," Aurnou has correctly observed; her love for Tarnower was a "magnificent obsession." Today, though, one wouldn't find it magnificent—just unhealthy—and would translate obsession as bondage. Living as we do without the historical perspective (a thirty-year-old woman I met had never heard of Betty Friedan), it's easy to forget that love has styles, that the Romantic Passion epitomized in the twelfth century by Tristan and Isolde—and today by Jean Harris—is bound for extinction.

The worst drawback to a Magnificent Obsession is that

it sets you up to take a lot of crap. Accept a situation not altogether on your terms. Like the mistress life, fourteen years of it.

Originally they planned to marry. There was even a big emerald-cut diamond. But after several months of engagement Tarnower called it off. He was afraid. He was sorry. He couldn't go through with it. Raising chutzpah to new heights, he somehow managed to make him*self* the victim—with her collaboration, alas. Jean worried about poor Hy, so backward, so Good Housekeeping, "thinking it's so bad, not marrying," thinking marriage "a requirement for middle-class respectability"—when "being married wasn't that important. Being with Hy was important." Refusing to see that Hy meant it, that by withholding marriage he *genuinely* withheld respect, that under the high-lifer was Babbitt. Refusing to see that you can't thumb your nose at convention à la Sartre and Simone de Beauvoir in bourgeois Westchester County. The danger of a Magnificent Obsession is that it keeps a woman as smart as Harris from smelling a rotten deal.

The mistress life had compensations of course. The logs kept by Suzanne van der Vreken, Tarnower's housekeeper (the only woman he would ever really need, said Harris when she returned the ring), record the holidays in Palm Beach, Paris, Kenya, Ceylon and other points around the globe. The flowered hostess gowns and satin evening shoes piled on the defense table are ghostly leavings from the round of posh parties. (And contrast tellingly with the polyester jackets of the working-class jurors.)

But what dues: composed of Special Occasions, the mistress life requires the stamina of an Amazon. How exhausting to be up to every occasion—suppose you want to be weekday humdrum, muck around in the valley. How tiring, after slogging away at work all week, to make the five-hour commute from McLean, Virginia, to Purchase, New

York. (Like in college romances, but who at eighteen had a demanding job or needed sleep?) The frightening exhaustion Harris felt, a classic symptom of depression, must also have come from her peripatetic life.

And a mistress is always auditioning: Am I still lovely? Are *we* still lovely? Am I still wanted? Still desirable? (Even with the flu, or fresh from the periodontist, or my mother in the nursing home, or any bout with reality?) A mistress is auditioning even if she doesn't covet a permanent role, because the liaison can be thrown into question at any juncture; it is renegotiable week by week. Symbolic of Harris's status is the *one drawer* Tarnower allotted her in his bedroom.

Then there are the other women. It is hard to get a fix on the Diet Doc's Astounding Appetite, in tabloid parlance, but Harris's close friend Marjorie Jacobson has testified that Harris would "rather travel with Hy and company than not all"—suggesting a floating entourage of "alternates" for whenever the head mistress was busy being headmistress. Lynne Tryforos became more than an alternate—another hazard of the mistress life. In recent years the doctor directed their arrivals and departures with the cool expertise of an air traffic controller. Once while Tarnower and Harris are on vacation, Tryforos razor-slashes her rival's clothes. There's worse: Somehow Lynne smears excrement on Jean's yellow silk dress. To a certain segment of the public this spectacle of two ladies slashing and smearing confirms what the gals are *really*, har har, about.

Harris accepted the other women—and the attendant horrors—because the only thing that mattered was "being with Hy." If those were his terms, she "would have to live with it." This is disturbing stuff. It is disturbing because the "it" Harris lived with is not some minor wart, like sucking teeth or repeating a limp joke. Fourteen years with a hard-core philanderer is a fourteen-year assault on your self-esteem—enough to fit it for the scrap heap. It is disturbing because this accomplished, witty woman, magna cum laude from Smith and dubbed Big Woman by her adoring sons, was powerless, as if stung by some evil spell, to act in her own self-interest. With occasional glimmers of insight, she saw her constancy as "masochistic"—but to no avail. Even toward the end, when he wished her out of his life, *she* wished—are you ready?—there were "many more ways I could do things for you."

And then it is disturbing, too, because—why not admit it?—the reformed masochists among us once lived it, took it, swallowed it and rationalized it. Harris's fourteen year stint is a more virulent grotesque version of our own sexual casualties. Only compared to her, we realize with a shudder, we were rank amateurs.

You could argue, I suppose, like a reporter I talked to during recess, that on some level Harris welcomed and fostered their mutual "independence." In Tarnower's bedroom hung a picture of a marionette she gave him, with the legend: "There are no strings on me." One could cite her jesting attitude toward Hy and his "broads," her tendency to cast him as Peck's Bad Boy ("Practically everything in his house was hemstitched, embroidered or engraved with women's names on it.") One could cite her assertion under oath that she didn't require marriage, that she knew "Hy was not a marrying man."

My guess: In her early forties she may well have liked the idea of No Strings. She was feeling experimental, daring, young—because after many years in Grosse Pointe With Strings, she had broken out, she was starting fresh. And from Go there was something deliciously illicit about the whole affair. Why force something so unique into the Grosse Pointe mold; why not Separate and Equal? And even with No Strings there were *rules*: He might collect bimbos by the barrelful, but he was not socially obligated to them; he would not publicly humiliate her; the bimbos had a place in his bed, but not in Their Crowd.

Later, though, in her fifties, independence must have felt increasingly to Jean Harris like *insecurity*. Of course there was plenty of admiration and support for women living in the adult No Strings mode—if not from stuffy Madeirans, from sophisticated Easterners. But it is easier to cheerlead from the sidelines than it is to be out in the field playing the game yourself. Playing the game yourself is exhausting and she couldn't hack it anymore, not without the pills. And by bringing Lynne to *their* old haunts, among *their* friends, Hy was breaking all the rules. However Jean Harris may have rationalized it in the beginning, I don't believe in her soul she liked No Strings. What woman born before 1950 would? Or man, for that matter? Who would elect to live without the most basic security? Un-chic though it may be in the Age of Autonomy, is not the need for security an honorable need?

"He slept with every woman he could. I have been through so much hell with him. I wanted to die," Jean Harris later told a policeman.

Why stay until it came to that? The man was *irreplaceable* was why. Anyone born before 1950, having felt that about someone herself, will recognize a *generational* fallacy, on its way to extinction. Today's young careerist invests achievement, her own, with the mystique Harris and company gave to The One. If shabbily treated, she moves briskly On To The Next, or simply over and out, secure in the belief that not only is there life after love, there is prosperity; there is self-respect. Nor would this pragmatic person, whom I admire and do not altogether resemble, harbor Harris's delusion that *she herself* was irreplaceable.

And then there were fourteen years of "promises"—"My home is your home, darling." "Welcome home, darling" —*that* can keep a woman in place. And narcotizing habit:

Every day she stayed it got harder to leave. And the life, so lovely, the sybaritic rituals dulling the fear that a younger body might replace the irreplaceable. Here too is the woman of a receding generation: the Kept Woman, you have to call it, no matter how proud Jean Harris was —they lived in a style *he* could afford. Such arrangements may be doomed: The cushy life which Tarnower bought her, which men have always bought women, women increasingly can buy on their own.

And then she must have gambled. Though well maintained, Tarnower was nearing seventy—the moment for even a man of his drives to take himself off the circuit, if only to avoid ridicule, if only to avoid a coronary; the moment for growing up, for even the inveterate bachelor to subside, grumbling happily, into matrimony. Until Harris saw Lynne Tryforos looming large in the wings, eager and willing to usurp the role Harris hoped for herself, it was a good risk; she thought she had time on her side.

In her mid-fifties now, what were her options? Not nearly so brilliant as the doctor's. At sixty-nine his life was expanding in every direction: He had his practice, honors, celebrity and riches from the diet book; unlimited social opportunities; the devotion of a woman thirty years his junior. He also had, if less often, his slave. And the support, even admiration, of many peers, unoffended by his juggling of two women. As one shruggingly explained, "Both women took it"; Tarnower was "in the catbird seat."

I imagine Harris's desolation at seeing many joint "friends" expediently switch their allegiance to Lynne. And her elder son was marrying—they were all leaving. *Her* life, Harris must have felt, was shrinking. Like most women of fifty-six she was not, one imagines, deluged with offers of marriage and romance—though of course she was handicapped by an appalling self-image, perceiving herself through her lover's eyes as "old and pathetic." And what she perceived as *his* luster (difficult to conceive from the photos) must have spoiled her for some perfectly nice Washingtonian, a gentleman, but so, well, *drab.*

Okay, but she had work. This much-touted job as head-mistress of the Madeira School, the "plum" of her profession. Let's look at this plum.

In choosing secondary-school education, Jean Harris chose a typical path to upward mobility open to women of her generation and class. The work was in the nurturing, helping mode, ladylike and unthreateningly low on the economic scale. In a sense it was the modern-day equivalent of the governess jobs sought in the nineteenth century by resourceful young women without means. Make no mistake, despite her chilly grace, diction and snobbishness, Harris was hardly the "socialite" of the tabloids, but from a "comfortably middle-class" background. (Though the expression is obsolete, who in the middle class today, that downwardly mobile group, feels comfortable?) She later wrote the doctor, who presumably didn't know, or didn't care, "I desperately needed money all these years."

Her Madeira "plum" paid $20,000. (A previous job paid $12,000; in the genteel, rarefied world of the private girls' school, the joy of forming young minds is considered the primary reward.) Of course Harris would have managed on the twenty thou (which came to more when you include housing and institutional meals)—but with a steep adjustment downward: no more Lyford Cay, Paris at the Ritz or African safaris. When women in her bracket lose the man, they lose the whole life, because the man underwrote the life. In Harris's case there is a sour footnote: "I have grown poor loving you," she wrote—having made *him* richer by toiling on his diet book.

Jean Harris, and women in my generation, too, younger

by some fifteen years, got caught short. We failed to or-
ganize our work lives around the solo scenario—like today's
careerist, who aspires to more than $20,000 by age fifty-six,
partly because not discounting the eventuality of ending
up alone. We envisaged our jobs as second incomes, the
man's being the primary. Then comes a divorce, a death,
a betrayal—and this job that fit the earlier scenario so well
is painfully out of phase with our needs and appetites.

But did Jean's plum at least provide other satisfactions?
Posh Madeira may have been a romp for the girls with
trust funds and monogrammed shetlands, but the head-
mistress has a twenty-four-hour job in which she is per-
petually on display. Self-enclosed and separate, and in the
case of Madeira physically isolated as well, it is a world of
official functions, hardly ideal for a woman seeking social
reentry. Ironically, Harris the snob, who applauded her
lover's snobbishness and despised Lynne's lack of class, was
herself not considered quite top-drawer at Madeira. She
was less a social equal of the trustees and parents than a
glorified governess, licensed for an arbitrary period to control access to this exclusive club. Caught in a crossfire from
enraged students, indignant parents and a high-handed
Board that limited her powers without explanation, she
was resigned to giving up this plum—and with it her last
shot at self-respect.

The weakest part of Harris's defense, though, is that the
debacle at Madeira made her suicidal. Certainly it was
desolating—but of a magnitude to inspire suicide? If people let their job miseries get to them, half the population
would hang themselves in the closet. That Harris felt suicidal I wouldn't dispute, but it was because she was losing
Tarnower too. "Look, Jean—it's your problem. I don't
want to hear about it," she imagines him saying. When
the job and the man go in one blow, it's the apocalypse.

Consider this scenario: At the height of the flak, Tarnower turns to Harris and says: "What do you need that crap for? I'm here for you. Come live with me, cool your heels for a while, there's always another job (etc., etc.— every woman, though she may never have heard them, can write the lines of the *mensch*). Obviously Harris is still frustrated, disappointed and mad as all hell—but it is all down to scale. Sorry. That despair and inability to cope was triggered by the absence of the Man to bail her out. Built into some corner of many a No Strings woman is the expectation that if it doesn't all work out, daddy—or somebody—will put up the bail.

Recklessly insisting on the primacy of love at any price, she lived out every woman's worst potential. She is, I suppose, an anti-role model. But Jean Harris will not easily leave us alone because of the larger lesson. Her adventure mocks the liberated pieties of people who believe that social attitudes have kept pace with women's aspirations. For fourteen years Harris and her lover lived outside tradition as independent "equals"—so adult, so evolved—yet in the twilight of that affair they hardly came out equal. Tarnower ended up with money, prestige, social opportunities and a devoted young mistress to grace his twilight years. And Harris ended up with little money, unemployment, dwindling social opportunities and the conviction that at fifty-six her life as a woman was over. Lacking a vocation for spinsterhood and self-abnegation, she believed her *life* over. Put melodramatically, you could say she ended up with nothing. Hers is a cautionary tale without consolations. I pity the men and women of the jury who judge her.

Promises Promises:
In Praise of Jean Harris

When the jury found Jean Harris guilty of murder in the second degree, I felt queasily despondent. Not terribly surprised though.

I had attended some of the trial on a magazine assignment, the standard female pro-Harris bias in tow. But on account of those multiple shots I had never bought the "tragic accident" scenario. I wondered at my splayed attitude: I don't as a rule condone murder; and I had to acknowledge that, obeying the judge's instructions not to let "sympathy" interfere, the jury probably had perpetrated justice.

So why did I feel so strong a solidarity with Mrs. Harris?

Partly out of rudimentary compassion, of course. How grisly to see a person as bruised and wasted as Harris, in that stoop that grew progressively more concave, "remanded" to custody—the very term crushes the spirit—and delivered into the penal machinery. Whose heart would not go out to that woman in the tabloid photo, eyes hunted and dazed behind the police car grille?

But unlike a majority of enlightened women who have judged her guilty of betraying the female sex and of masochism in the first degree, I also admire Jean Harris. She clung pitiably to an abusive man; certainly she was never the exemplary feminist heroine. Still, in happier times she displayed a rare adventuresomeness, engineering a life of love and work far beyond the safe confines of convention.

This coolish woman with an outsize passion must have dispassionately assessed her alternatives: Having sent back Tarnower's ring, she could "live her own life" with the reasonable expectation of meeting up with a marrying, if lesser, man (in the "Letter" she hints at concrete prospects). Or she could, in a different sense, live her own life as traveling mistress-in-residence to a man she adored (and did not reflexively consider expendable—he's okay, but so is *he* okay—as prescribed by today's mental health pragmatists).

In choosing her course, surely she must have factored in the sacrifices and risks: She would not have security, money and the "Good Housekeeping seal" accorded a wife. But by cultivating her own garden she would create a modest financial security. And because she offered more than Hy's ubiquitous "broads," and because of his "promises," tantamount to vows, she could enjoy a measure of emotional security. And though it was all a bit dicey, there being more precedents in Paris than Westchester for this brand of alliance, and she would be winging it, improvising as she went, she would have something that many wives in Westchester did not.

For a forty-three-year-old woman in prefeminist 1967, with two young children, a lousy-paying job and no financial backup, this choice took the daring of a Lindbergh in the *Spirit of St. Louis.*

She crash-landed, of course. But it is too easy to say, with hindsight, that she picked the wrong sort of life with the wrong sort of guy; too easy to point out, with hindsight, that given Tarnower's proclivities, neither her achievements nor devotion could argue, finally, against a twenty-years-younger body. Too easy to observe, with hindsight, that a man and woman keep company for fourteen years, independent and "equal," but don't necessarily end up equal.

Harris's critics are also a bit quick, it seems to me, to dismiss her devotion to Tarnower as love-slobbism, or some related female pathology. True, love is generally in disrepute and considered in many quarters an exercise in self-destructiveness (novelist Beryl Bainbridge recently reduced it to "flu-like symptoms"). But at a time when everyone is busy Getting Theirs, looking out for Number 1 or dickering over premarital contracts, is there not something refreshing and grand about a gratuitous passion that required no goods, no fringe benefits, nothing beyond the beloved's company? The nineteenth century generally, and the novelist Stendhal in particular, would have celebrated precisely the qualities in Harris that today's pragmatists deplore—her incautiousness, unstintingness, her great-heartedness (her *"espagnolisme,"* the highest praise in Stendhal's canon). Jean Harris was all too guilty, clearly, of being an anachronism.

But also, of course, of intending to kill—which raises again the irksome question: Granted, Harris had guts—but isn't supporting her tantamount to condoning murder?

Let's sweep off the board those crazies who flocked to the courthouse ranting, "The bastard got what he deserved." Harris's less frenetic advocates (and they include men) are saying something of a different order. While not precisely recommending that a faithless lover be brought low with a bullet through the clavicle, neither do they feel that a lover who has behaved despicably should stroll into the sunset with impunity. In the uncomfortable space in between, Harris's supporters are insisting, rather, on the need for moral obligation—a need that may well differentiate humans from, say, baboons.

I hear the objections: Tarnower "owed" Harris nothing. As prosecutor Bolen phrased it in his closing rodomontade, "The doctor chose a bachelor life. . . . They had no marital bonds."

This is pernicious thinking, though. It implies that only "marital bonds" entail responsibility to the Other and curtail unstinting devotion to self. And let's decode a "bachelor life" as a privileged tax-free existence exempting a man from any obligation to his harem, serial or otherwise. (With touching largesse, Bolen extended the "bachelor" option to women, which should cheer those of us hoping to consort with a thirty-seven-year-old Boy Friday at age sixty-nine.)

What Harris supporters insist is that the prevailing philosophy of "I'm not responsible for you and you're not responsible for me" is dead wrong.

What Harris supporters insist is that Tarnower *did* owe her. I am not talking about palimony—though the concept of reimbursement for time invested in a lover's career is laudable. I am talking about a more elusive, more difficult indebtedness.

In Harris's words, the doctor "very carefully set out to be the most important thing" in her life. If we accept the notion that we are in some way obligated toward the person whose affections we have received, encouraged and nourished, and that the obligation increases with the duration of the affair—then Tarnower had accumulated one whopping debt. What form the acknowledgment of that debt should have taken I leave to the Rose Franzblaus, Joyce Brotherses and ethicists at large. Let us say that at the least the doctor was obliged to negotiate a satisfactory ending—though it cut into his hunting trips, though it disrupt his current amours. And that, having failed to do so, he became vulnerable to the perils besetting anyone in breach of faith.

To rally behind Harris is not to applaud murder, but rather to affirm the single socially redeeming value to emerge from this interminable trial: Between longtime lovers there exist unnotarized yet unbreachable "contracts," written not in ink, but in honor.